BROWNSHUGAR

YOLANDA HUGHES

Speak and live in simple sentences.

Bring closure – put a period to – those experiences

that you don't want to carry on forever and ever.

Use commas in those places where you're still growing.....

And use exclamation points at the end of the lesson.

~ Iyanla Vanzant

DEDICATION

I dedicate this book first to my hometown of Newark, New Jersey where I was born, raised and schooled in life. To my neighborhood of New Community Corporation, circa 1979 – 2004 where I was fortunate enough to grow up in a time when as children, we actually played outside until the lights came on, fights were won with fists, water or words and you lived to see another day. Video games were our past time only when it was too cold or too wet outside to play or because you were on punishment for one reason or another.

To Paul Reid and Sheila Washington (May she rest in peace), the first Summer Youth Directors at the community camp who were like black heroes to us back then. They were the first people outside our immediate families who showed us life outside our 'hood' and told us we were bigger than our circumstances; and we believed them.

To Little Joe's Bar for being our "club house" as young adults. Where everybody knew your nickname (LOL) and friendship woes were tested or mended over music spun by DJs Spinbad, Champ and Vic. [Champ and Vic thank you for always being available whenever I needed you but more importantly, when I didn't] And to the friends, family and foes of NCC. As Rahman would say… "NCC for life."

ACKNOWLEDGMENTS

To my siblings, Yvonne, Adrienne, Stephany, Kevin, Keith, Lawrence, Tomboy, Tyrone and may he forever rest in peace, Terry; my 16 other nieces and nephews, my Aunts Gloria, Beverly, Davonne and Barbara as well as my Uncles Butch, Robert and Harold. To my cousins and biggest cheerleaders, Karen, Sheila, Stacey, Lydia, Randi, Aneesa, Tia, Shadee, Francelle and Billy. And the remainder of the Hughes, Burks, LaMarr, Garrett and Williams Families. I could not have asked to be born into a better gang! I am always proud to acknowledge that I come from you.

Not wanting to forget or leave out the Burwell's/Colwell's; Deborah, Neal, Shonda, Na-Na and Shinequa. I know you know how much all of you have influenced my life since I was eight years old. Deb, you were always and still are my other-mother-sister-friend and I thank you all from the bottom of my heart for allowing me to be a part of your family. I've used your presence in my life to be of great example to others and I hope I made you proud.

Na-Na, I wanted to say to you especially that I would swear that no other person has put so much trust in their sibling as you have in me. I need for you to always know that every step I've made since you became my sister has been with you in mind. Good and bad, I've wanted to be of greater example for you as Deborah, Adrienne, Stephany and Yvonne have been too me. I work hard at making you proud to call me your big sister.

To Michelle Howard (Ro-Ro), I can't thank you enough for birthing the new love of my life, Teri, and giving me opportunity to be of influence on her. I love her life. And to my great friend

LaTonya "Stormy", who makes it her business to tell me often enough how beautiful I am inside and out on a regular basis and for a constant and steadfast confidant. I love you for that Girlie! As Pastor Johnson would say, our friendship makes my heart stand-up.

To Sharla… for believing and supporting every dream I've had since we met in college and being unwavering throughout. You are a beautiful sista with the insight to make all things happen and I'm trusting you will continue to be of great strengths and talents.

EBONY! Your picture was/is my inspiration... you're a beautiful muse and I can't wait to work with you more.

Janet Suggs! You are incredible. Your influence on one of the characters had changed the course of the book. Thank you isn't enough for your honesty and friendship.

My P2, Kisha Hudson! YOU have kept me excited about the characters and development of this book from the very beginning. If my immediate family members were the cheerleaders, then you were their coach. Thank you so much for the encouragement, lending your ear on the train rides to the city and for your honest opinions, reactions and questions. I love you Twin.

Tudy, Tudy, Tudy…. A 30+ friendship is hard to come by these days yet we haven't missed a beat with one another since we were eight years old. I look forward to the next 32 years and I thank you for supporting me.

Brooklyn, there is much I can say to you but nothing I haven't said to your face before. You gave me the inspiration to WRITE my story years ago and it took me a minute to put pen to paper. But I did it and you held me down as long as I sat at that computer. Not everyone could do what you did and so I'm thankful and grateful to you as well for your support and insight to the characters of this book.

And finally to my mother, the late Shirley Ann Burks whose love of books and reading I've inherited. Whose virtues and teachings have guided her entire family to be the prize-winning garden we are. I thank you Mommy for first watering the garden your mother left you, planting more rose buds along the way and for nurturing each one of us individually. Finally, I thank you for being my mother, my best friend and my idol. If I ever mature into half of who you were I will have conquered the world. I miss you deeply every day!

~ All my love,
Yogi

1 JOURNAL ENTRY
October 14, 1990

It's about 8:15 pm and Rick and I are walking from my house on Irving Street to his house on Priceland Avenue and I'm cute! LOL. I had on my Liz Claiborne jumpsuit from Lord & Taylor with my navy blue 2 ½ inch heels by Kenneth Cole with a brand new pair of name earrings spelling both my first and middle name; Cherise dangled from one ear and Shugar from the other.

Rick and I are laughing about something silly, enjoying the still warm weather as we are just getting ready to pass the old Ark school that is abandoned and looking like it will fall down at any minute; not really paying attention to the group of guys coming our way.

Just before passing them, Rick grabs my hand and pulls me off the sidewalk next to the empty lot behind the old school. He guides me into the street to let them pass to keep me from stepping onto the dirt and broken glass. He wanted me out of their way. Just as I go by the last guy in the group of seven, I feel my pocketbook being snatched off my arm and I'm immediately turned around by the force of the pull off my shoulder.

Rick reacts by turning around with me but he is still holding my hand. Before he can utter one word, his mouth is bust open by a steel pole to his face. I feel his hand tear away from mine as he falls to the ground. I go down to the ground with him and I'm realizing we are being robbed. I pray they take what they want and leave; but they don't.

The shortest of the seven guys yells at me… "Stand up bitch! Stand up! You hear me talking to you. That nigger can't do shit to help you now bitch." I turn around slowly on the balls of my feet. Crying, I stand up as slow as I could with my face down all the while clinching my fists in my hands. I'm thinking that I'm only about a block and half from home; I should try to run from these thugs. But what about Rick? Damn! They got my wallet with my whole paycheck in it; cash. Shit! Oh well, they got it now, I decided.

Just then, WHAP! A slap across my face by the male with very light colored eyes and the next thing I know, the top of my jumpsuit is ripped open and I'm staring in shock like "what the hell is happening?" I look back at Rick who is now standing about ten yards away from me in the empty lot with two of the men punching him in his head and yelling at him to watch what was about to happen to me as they hold him back.

WHAP! Another slap across my face and somebody is yelling for me to take my earrings and bracelet off but I'm in pure panic mode now. I'm frozen in place not moving at all while somebody else hits me in the back of my legs with a pipe. My knees buckled underneath me and I crash to the ground on my back. I'm dragged off into the dirt of the lot next to Rick with the bottom half of my very nice jumpsuit dragging underneath me. My shoes had somehow come off long before now and I'm barefoot. I feel the blood running down my nose and the back of my legs are burning as my thighs and heels of my feet are being shredded by the broken glass and rocks they have hauled me over.

As I lay on the cold ground with pieces of cardboard underneath me to protect my rapist's knees, half naked with only the arms of my jumpsuit still on my body, I look up and around at the people peeking out their windows and peering out their doors just across the street and it's quiet. Very still over there. Porch lights and room lights come on and off one by one and curtains are separated as I hear people whispering but no one is yelling to stop this assault except Rick who is getting his ass kicked at arms lengths away from me. He's begging them to wait for something and not to hurt me anymore, but to no avail. The assault continued on both of us and it's agonizing what they are doing to me.

My consciousness decides to check-out at this point and I began to stare up at the sky and wonder what is my mother going to think when she finds out what happened to me or what if one of my friends come down this street; would they stop to see what was happening or would they turn a blind-eye to it like the gutless voyeurs peeking out around me.

One by one, I'm being raped repeatedly by seven different men; I don't remember counting. Right there in a dirty lot filled with garbage and field mice trotting around us. I can hear my flesh being ripped apart by the sticks and bottles they are using to sodomize me for their amusement. I feel every thrust into me with their dirty penises but I can especially smell their sweaty skin and breaths. The stench of their hair and the feel of their eyelashes touching my cheeks as they take turns on top of me, shrinking me into nothing. I just lay there. Not even crying. Not moving; no attempts at trying to make them stop. One of them is biting my bare nipples so hard they bleed while another is forcing his entire fist into my vaginal cavity. His filthy grimy hand feels like hot boulders filling my belly with such vigor and fury that if I wasn't blocking this out mentally, I

3

would have passed out from the pain. But I'm numb as I picture the look in my sister's eyes when she sees my bloodied body after I'm found. I can only imagine what the funeral will be like; probably closed casket because these guys are pummeling me as they go back and forth raping my soul and planting seeds of self-doubt and self-hatred deep in my core.

Then I'm flipped over on my face and the few remnants of my panties are removed from my body as I'm assaulted anally. First with thumbs and then an attempt with a penis but I was too tight and it couldn't be forced in. Instead, I was turned back over on my back; face up. Still staring at nothing. It didn't register to me that I was being showered upon with hot piss to my face. Stinging every open cut and scape around my eyes and forehead. Suddenly, there is an especially forceful push into my body with something cold and bigger than a fist and it's making tiny slices on the lips of my vagina that are excruciating. My trance is broken and I begin to yell, "FIRE! FIRE! FIRE!" I'm reaching between my legs and I pull out the Pepsi can they were trying to shove up in me and I turn over on my stomach. "FIRE! FIIIRREEE! FIRE!"

All seven of them run in the direction they came; there's one with a short leg trailing in the back, and just like that… all it took was for me to yell, scream, shout out loud and they run like the punks they are. This revelation will haunt me later but I jump to my feet like a crazy person and begin to look for my shoes and in my blur I find my purse on the ground un-opened. The jewelry I took off was strewn around in the dirt as well. They didn't want it. I turn. I find one shoe and I put it on and realize I need to put my legs back into my jumpsuit; I don't have on underwear anymore. So I stop and do that; put my feet in one by one into the pants legs… and I'm calm but my body is still sedated to what just happened. I don't feel anything. I guess I'm what they call in-shock; moving robotically around the lot looking for pieces of me to put back together. But I'm scared because I am still alive and I have to tell my Mom what happened here. She is going to be very upset with me.

Just then, some woman appears in the lot alongside me and gently puts a blanket around my shoulders and is guiding me across the street by my wrist to her porch, but where is Rick I think. I don't even remember the walk across the street. I'm like in a warp zone and nothing is making good sense at that moment. This woman sits me down on the folding chair that's positioned outside her window and the shade inside her home is still parted where she once stood witnessing my transformation to innocent young girl to victim. She is saying something about the police and an ambulance and how she saw everything… blah, blah, blah and I look up and see a crowd of people forming around me but I don't see Rick. Where is Rick?

The crowd's roaring whisper is loud but very hushed at the same time. I don't speak. There is a foul salty taste in my mouth and I want to spit but my mother would say it's not ladylike so I don't.   Someone is pushing through the crowd forming around the porch making a beeline for me. "Oh SHIT! Shugg? What the fuck happened?" He turns around, "Who the fuck did this to my sister?" Which one of you mother fuckers did this to my sister?" he is yelling at the top of his lungs and I force myself to focus on his voice. "I have to get out of this foggy head I'm in," I think. It's Ethan! Oh God! It's Ethan!

I leap up and bury my face in my brothers back as he is screaming and crying tears of anger and disgust. And I'm grabbing at his waist and hands from behind trying to hide my sudden embarrassment in his body somehow and I'm crying for my brother to hold me and he does. My eldest brother turns and puts his arm around my shoulder. He pulls me away from the folding chair and under his arms and I follow him off the porch with just one shoe and my purse all the while holding pieces of my clothes together to cover my badly bruised body. I am desperate to cover my breast that are leaking blood from being bitten and chewed and I haul my exposed chest and legs, that feel mutilated, into the back seat of his car.

I'm no longer numb to the aches and pains of my body. I'm abruptly aware of my unconcealed flesh and realize my tattered under garments are somewhere in the lot across the street. I'm cold and shivering and my face begins to hurt and the blood is stinging my eyes.

The chilly leather seats make me cognizant that my skin hurts too and that my arm is limp against my body. I can tell it's broken. Ethan is hushing me as tears pour out of his eyes. He takes off his hooded shirt and wets a sleeve with spit from his mouth to wipe the white crusted secretion around my own. I notice the disgust in his eyes as he recognizes what the substance is and it is hurting him more as he begins to understand moment by moment the magnitude of what happened to his sister. Me. It hurts him to look at my engorged eyes that were now swollen shut along with a busted lip and two broken teeth.

Ethan soothingly puts my head on the blanket the woman put around my shoulders on his lap as someone else drives us to my mother's house… only a block and a half away. And still I wonder where Rick is?

2 JOURNAL ENTRY
July 1, 1994

Rushing home from work on this ridiculously hot ass summer day, I pull up in the parking lot of our townhouses at like 25 miles an hour, dying to get out of this damn car and into my bedroom under an air conditioner, I notice these teenagers playing in the lot again, blocking my parking spot. Oh well, it'll be 10 points if I hit one of them with this car. "MOVE!" I yell at the tall dark-skinned boy with his stupid-ass-4 sizes too big- jean jacket wearing-and wool-skull-in-the-summer-time self. Dang! He makes me sick with his slow bopping ass. Always outside sitting in the parking lot staring at me whenever I come in and out. I just recently started noticing him around but Kyra said he's been living in the neighborhood for a while now. I guess I just never noticed him before. Doesn't matter. He's just some young kid out here smoking and drinking like the rest of the retards he hangs out with.

I grab my heels, purse and keys from the passenger seat of my 325i royal blue BMW and stepped my tall 5' 11", 163 pound mocha brown frame out of the car, forcing my barely-there hips and little round butt up and down and side to side as smooth as I can to my mother's house because I know these young boys are watching. Especially that dark-skinned one; he always checking for me.

"Shugar! Yo Shugar! You left your sun roof open!" he yelled at me as I stepped onto the porch to my mother's back door. See what I mean? Why he even paying that kind of attention to what I'm doing anyway? "Dats alright", I yelled back without even turning around. "I'ma be leaving back out in a little while anyway. Don't be sitting all over my car though."

I walked past my mother cooking in the kitchen and went straight to my room on the second floor of our townhouse where my pretty little angel was fast asleep taking her afternoon nap as always. I lean down and kiss those chubby cute little cheeks of hers as I brush one of her pigtails out of her face. Her hand is still clenching the blue crayon she used to draw me this picture of I-don't-know-what that is lying on the floor next to the bed. To be only four years old, Stormy is a very talented young lady. Just staring at that face makes me want to cry because she is the most beautiful thing in my life in spite of…. Well, never mind. I hate to think about that when I'm looking at her. Good thoughts! Good thoughts!

I rise from the bed and checked my bedroom door to see if one of my brothers attempted to get in my room while I was at work and before my Mom laid my baby down. COOL. My air conditioner had turned on automatically about 1 hour ago while I was still at work and this space was going to be my heaven for at least the next 3 hours.

I leaned across my water bed, careful not to wake my angel and peered out the window to see if those kids were leaning on my car anyway after I warned them not too. Yep!

So disrespectful. I wasn't concerned because I knew one of my brothers would be pulling up soon enough and they would make them get off my car. Once Jamil, Jamaal or Ethan told them to do something or not to do something, respect was given and I wouldn't have to worry about it again. At least not until the next day anyway.

But I'm noticing that dark-skinned one dropping a piece of folded paper through my sunroof onto my passenger seat. Maybe a receipt or something fell when I was getting out the car. Oh well. I'll see what it is later when I leave out to hang with Sincere downtown in front of the Dream Bar.

I hopped in the shower real quick and changed into a pair of jeans with my nickname spray painted down the front leg. BrownShugar in neon pink and green. My mom would always call me her 'brown sugar cube' whenever I did something to please her. Plus it incorporated my middle name, Shugar and so; nice attribute, I always thought. I find the matching slouch socks and neon pink t-shirt with my white-on-white Reebok Classics. Then I paged Sincere with 911 and waited for him to call me back and tell me what time to meet him or if he will pick me up. In the meantime, I checked the messages on my voicemail and watched MTV until the moment arrived to do one thing or the other.

Message 1 at 3:15 pm: "Hey Shugar! It's Tiesha. Call me when you get home from work. I wanna know if I can borrow your car to meet up with Hector at Ihop in Glen Ridge for a few minutes at 6. Love you Auntie. Bye."

She must be stupid thinking I'ma let her drive my whip around. I don't even let my brothers drive it unless they paying me too.

Message 2 at 3:46 pm: "Yo. It's Bilal. Page me when

you get home. I'm thinking about you spending the night at my crib and you finally letting me get a lil bit. I mean damn. What do a brother gotta to do to get a lick? Sike. I know you hate when I talk like dat. Respect. But seriously page me or call me at the barbershop. Peace."

This guy! When I had a crush on him in high school he would call me Skinny Minnie and tell me I looked like an olive branch. Now, five years later since graduating high school, he interested? Puhleaze!! Besides, I don't do drug-dealers. I get enough grief living with them under the same roof. I'm not tryna have one as a boyfriend.

Message 3 at 4:01 pm: "Hey Baby. I'm on my way to class and wanted to tell you that I'm coming home for the weekend. I'm catching a ride with Beau and Barbara and should get to your house by like 4 am. If your mother made spaghetti, can you put me some in a bowl and save it for me? Love you. Bye."

Rick! I love me some Rick…. He is my first real boyfriend and the first person to tell me I was pretty or sexy or anything remote to making me feel like an attractive woman. Rick is my first everything really. My first real tongue kiss, first sexual partner and he was the first and only person I will ever allow to go down on me. More importantly, he's a college graduate and I hope we stay together and get married one day. But for now I know he doing it to those girls down at Howard. But so what. He loves me and our baby and that is all that matters. By the time I get back from chillin' with Sincere he should be here. I can't wait.

Hours later, Sincere picks me up from in front of my door and it's off to party until 3 am. When I arrive back home, I check my messages again and I hear Mrs. Marshall's voicemail that she and Pop-Pop picked Stormy up from my mom earlier so that they can spend time with her before their son Rick arrived and that she just needs me to drop her swimsuit for their play date tomorrow. No problem I think. Then I crash onto my bed and just lay there from the sheer exhaustion of dancing and partying all night. I had so much fun… but Rick isn't here yet. I think I'm gonna take a shower and go to sleep. I'll catch up with him by morning.

POP! POP! POP! POP! POP! I can smell the gun powder waft through my second floor bedroom window and I dare not move for a few seconds but then I think of my brothers and those shots came from right underneath my window. So I roll onto my belly and peer out the window in time to see someone picking up something from the ground around my back door. The back porch light is on and I recognize him! More importantly, I notice the big silver gun in his hand I dare not even take a breath in fear he'll notice me in the window and shoot at me. But he runs in the opposite direction he was firing and I release a long exhale.

I look over towards where my car was parked in the direction he was aiming and there she was underneath the spotlight of the street light….her body was still twitching. I can only remember she had on money green leggings and matching sneakers, positioned in a pool of her own blood as if she was running in place before that bullet pierced her skull and stopped her cold in her tracks. The makeshift table in front of her was knocked over and the crates they were sitting on as chairs were spewed all over the parking lot they were playing cards in. It was dead silent now and as my mom and I race down the stairs from our bedrooms and out the back door towards her. As we approached, you can almost feel the spirit leave Mimi's 18 year old body as she takes her last breath.

Off in the distance, you hear the friends she was playing cards with descending back to where they all ran off in different directions when the shots began to ring out. They are laughing and talking loud about hearing the shots but not knowing where they were coming from. The took pride in outrunning the inevitable danger of guns not yet realizing that their friend was lying dead in the same spot they left her; just 10 short minutes ago.

JOURNAL ENTRY
July 13, 1994

I'm just coming back home from dropping changing clothes off to Rick's mom for Stormy and the parking lot where my car was still parked is taped up and so many people are standing around with the local newspaper interviewing Mimi's aunt and uncle about her murder the night before. There are candles burning around a makeshift memorial where she died and her friends are all just sitting around saying and doing nothing.

My mom is on the porch as I approach and as she begins to ask about how Stormy was doing with her other grandparents; we turn our heads towards the loud wailing that is coming towards us. We look, and the tall dark-skinned boy who is always outside checking for me is crying like his very essence aches. Ibin is walking towards the memorial and I think he is in pain considering the noise escaping his mouth. I thought maybe he got shot or something and my Mom begins to instinctively descend off the porch, like mother's do, with her arms out to embrace him as he approaches. Protectively, I follow my mother to this young man myself to see what was going on and all he could say is, "this is fucked up man! They killed her for NOTHING! This is fucked up." Wow, was my only thought. Who is "they" that killed her? And why did "They" do it?

I steer he and my mother to our porch and walked them both into my mother's dining room as she shuffles off to get him a glass of water. I sit at the table with him and takes his hand in mine and ask his name. "Ibin" he replied. "Ibin, are you okay?" I ask cautiously. He tries hard to compose himself as my mom sits the glass of water in front of him and takes the other seat across from me. "It's just fucked up what happened to Mimi last night. (He catches his own disrespect) Oh shit. I'm sorry Ms. Brown. I don't mean to curse in front of you." My mom pats him on the back and tells him it's okay and that she understands.

"It's just that we was just sitting outside last night playing cards and listening to music and next you know, POP! POP! POP! (He motions with his fingers) Somebody starts shooting from somewhere and we run in all different directions not knowing that they was aiming for our ass. Den... we thinking Mimi right behind us running towards the avenue or to her house or something but she caught a bullet to her eye man. Dat's fucked up man. She didn't have to die like that." Then he looks me straight in my eyes and asks, "Why she have to die like that on that cold ground wit nobody around Shugar?"

Damn. I can't answer that. I don't even know her and before just now, I didn't even know his name. But I reply, "It's just the way God wants it be. It was her time to go. Whatever God's reason, she didn't die in vain and you can't dirty up her memory by doing something stupid like killing somebody else in her honor. You understand Ibin?" I wasn't sure of what I was saying but I know how people are these days with guns and its likely there will be more shots fired in the days and nights to come.

My mother interrupts his stare into my eyes and asks is there anything she can do to help and he shakes his head no. He doesn't let my hand go and I don't try to take it away. I feel Ibin's sad energy surging through the connection in our hands and I'm intrigued by it for some reason. It's more to him than this incident. There is anger in his face and I recognize that emptiness as I am drawn to know more…. and I will.

The next couple of days are the same with local news reporters in our backyard asking the normally drama free community about the recent incidents of gun shots and retaliation for the murder of Milly Washington. The candles still burned on the side walk and the pictures of Mimi were taped to the gates surrounding the lot or on large pieces of cardboard that was affixed to the ground where here head once laid. But the crime-scene ribbon had been removed and cars were able to park again in their respective assigned spots.

One day as I arrive home in the late evening, I fully expect what has become the new norm of a crowd of people outside discussing the incident. I'm surprised when I only see Ibin and his mother, Mona. As I begin to take my daughter out of the backseat and her daddy, Rick, removes her baby bag and toys from the floor surrounding her, I make a conscious effort to acknowledge Ibin and say hello. Only to notice that Ibin was waving hello back but staring at Rick with such intensity that instantly, I'm uncomfortable with the scene. Thankfully, Rick doesn't notice as he comes around the car to take Stormy out of my arms and carries her into my house.

Mona hits Ibin on his arm to get his attention and break his trance as I'm walking up to him to ask what the fuck his problem was staring at my man like that. "Ibin? What was that about? Do you know Rick or something?" I ask with distaste on my tongue to match his annoyed face. "Nah." He replied. "But is that your man?" he asked. "Yes it is but can I ask why are you staring at him like he stole something from you?" I say. Just then, Mona steps between our exchange and wraps her boney fingers around my forearm and looks up at me and says, "It's nothing Doll. Ibin just trippin' cause your man looks like somebody he knows that's all." She looks up at Ibin and grits her teeth at him and says, "Right Ibin?" He doesn't reply at all. Ibin just looks past me at my back door.... "Ok. Well, whatever." I say and turn my back to the both of them and continue in the house myself.

Later that evening, after my daughter was asleep, Rick and I leave my house so that I can take him back home to his parent's home where he will be leaving before dawn to drive back to Howard to finish a required summer class that was needed to earn his diploma. Rick had participated in the actual graduation ceremony a few months earlier but because he had to repeat a class, his diploma would be dependent on him re-taking that class and passing.

Ibin and his crew were outside but no odd exchanges happened between he and Rick and I was relieved. But when I returned home an hour or so later there was only Ibin; sitting outside on my back porch at 12:05 in the morning, smoking a fat blunt waiting on my arrival.

"How you just gonna sit on my mother's porch smoking that shit underneath my window being disrespectful? How do you know my daughter's not home inhaling all that poison you sucking down your throat?" I asked with my foot on the step between Ibin's Timberland boots.

Ignoring my questions and without looking up he says, "I don't mean you no disrespect but is that dude you was

16

with your serious boyfriend or just somebody you fucking?"
"WHAT!" I barked on this person I considered a young boy.
"Who the hell do you think you talking too little BOY? You
don't know me to be asking me no shit like that. Sitting on
my porch smoking those funny cigarettes tryna be grown.
Get up off my porch with that bullshit. And just because I
was nice enough to share a few conversations with you and I
pay your young ass a little attention, don't authorize you to
think you know me well enough to question me or talk to me
like you on my level. You do NOT know Shugar Brown!"

In a low but very controlled voice, Ibin replied, "I may
not know you yet Shugar Brown, but I do know a punk when
I see one. And that niggah you was with earlier is a straight
up punk. Ain't no thorough niggah I know gonna let a little
BOY; that's what you called me right? Ice grill him like I
did a little while ago without catching a serious beat down.
So, I sat my boyish ass right here on your porch and waited
for you to come back just so I could tell you to your face that
your man is a punk and I don't want him around you or your
daughter any more. Not only that. (He takes a pull off his
blunt) After what I heard about that punk, he gotta ass-
whooping coming to him anyway for what he DIDN'T do to
protect you. But I know you got your reasons for letting that
ride. Add that to the fact that you think you tough and you
gonna do what you want to do as far as he concerned, I'ma
just say, he ain't allowed in this neighborhood no more.
Period. How about that Ms. Shugar Brown?"

This boy must've lost his mind I'm thinking, but I laugh
at him to ensure he has not gotten the best of me with his
little antics. Telling me who I can and cannot see. Who can
and cannot come into the neighborhood. That's my

daughter's father he talking about and Rick ain't no punk!

"Whatever little man. That MAN you are referring to is my daughter's father for your information. Just stay out of grown folks business. Anyway, get off my porch and go see about your mother wondering around over there looking to score a bag of dope." I say with such venom on my tongue I hope it stings him as much as his words stung me.

"Okay Shugar." Ibin says as he stands up and steps down off the porch looking me up and down and grinning. He towers over me and bends forward to plant a kiss on my forehead and walks away towards his mother. But then he turns around briefly and ends his assault on my ego with, "By the way….. the note I left in your car is true."

I run up to my room and slam the door angry. Not caring at all if my daughter or mother is awakened by my reaction to Ibin's nonsense. Seriously! I don't know who he thinks he is. And what's up with the kiss to my forehead? He must be mental.

I peek out my window and watch Ibin shuffle his mother towards their apartment and disappear behind the darkness. I'll deal with his ass next time.

A couple of weeks go by and I avoid this Ibin character like he's a plague. I leave to work earlier than normal, I come home later, I change my parking spot and instead of coming in out of the back door, I start using the front door. I have no words for him and I don't have time for any more of his insults. Besides, this neighborhood is getting worse by the minute and I gotta concentrate on getting me, my mom and daughter out of here as soon as possible.

Just my luck, as I'm sneaking out the front door again

pretending to be reading my sky pager messages intently while walking to my car, I look up in time to see one of my brothers, Jamil, talking to Ibin in front of my parked car.

"Shugggggggg" my brother sings as I am pressing the automatic unlock on my keychain so I can jump in and peel off. "I was just telling my man Ibin that I was gonna ask you if I can use your ride real quick to make a run to Messiah Courts for a pick-up. I promise it will take us 20-25 minutes tops and I'll give you $100 when I come baccckkk.....?? Okay Sister?"

"Nope" was my immediate reply. "Now move outta my way. I have stuff I have to do Jamil."

"C'mon Shugar. Me and Ibin gonna come right back. You know I can't use my car for that". Jamil says, still pleading"

I was gonna say something about how he figures it's not a good idea to use his car but it was a good idea to use mine but then Ibin suspends my thought and says, "Nah Mill. Let Shugar take care of her business and take her car. I'ma ask my man Rock to run us over there real quick cause that's his hood and that way it ain't no issues with them niggahs worrying about a suspicious car in their woods. You feel me?"

"Oh. Okay then". Jamil says. "That'll work".

With my hand, I kindly move Jamil over from blocking my car door and climb in behind the wheel. As I'm turning over the ignition, Jamil taps the glass and motions for me to roll down the window.

"Shug. What's up with Rick? I haven't seen him down here for a minute and he told me he graduated last month. I need to holla at him for something. Yall aight?" Jamil says to me with a questionable look on his face.

And I couldn't help but peek over Jamil's shoulder at Ibin who just winked his eye at me and then has the nerve to give me thumbs up sign as he is clearly ear hustling our conversation. I roll my eyes up in my head at Ibin and reply to Jamil, "he's been busy working at his new job downtown and looking for a place for us to move too. He'll be back around. Just give him a minute to get his situation in order."

Before I allowed my brother to turn this conversation into something more, I motion for him to get out of the way of my car and I drive off. UGGHHHH... I really don't like this Ibin character. I hope he don't think Rick hasn't been coming around because of his little empty threat. Little does he know, I told Rick to worry about getting his business in order and I'll come to his parent's house to chill with him and Stormy as opposed to him coming to my Mom's house all the time. Plus; he always says he's tired everyday coming home from work. I don't want him to be running back and forth over here to be with me and Stormy when we could just as easily go there. That's why I'm going there now. To be with them; my family. Humph!

As I arrive, Rick doesn't even notice me pulling up to his parent's home because he's so engrossed in a conversation with some chick who looks like she is coming from inside the house. Smiling at her with one hand on her waist, he leans in and whispers something in her ear that makes her dimples appear and her size 40DD breasts jiggle up and down. So I beep the horn to get his attention and they both jump as they finally observe me parking.

Sashaying her big butt and curves past me as I approach Rick standing in the doorway, the very attractive young lady says to me, "Hi Shugar. I'm done with your man now. By the way, your little girl is gorgeous. I've never seen anyone with one green and one hazel eye before. It's funny because neither you nor her daddy have eyes like that. You should put her in commercials with her sweet self." Then turns towards Rick and with slick grin says, "Good night Rick. I will call you when I get home."

Really?!

3 JOURNAL ENTRY
January 20, 1995

New year, new problems I'm thinking as I'm phoning
Rick AGAIN today to tell him he needs to make sure he
pays for Stormy' s dance class lessons and either takes her to
try on the ballet slippers she needs or give me the money to
go and buy them myself. However, it's sounding like I'm
going to have to leave a message with that very thought
because he is still not answering his phone.

This is the fourth day in a row I've called, left him
messages for him at work and at home just to have his
mother call me back with his replies or him ignoring me all
together. I can afford to pay for Stormy's dance classes
myself but I shouldn't have too. He's working now and he
can pay his share to help me take care of our daughter. His
parents shouldn't have to do it anymore. Forget that! I'm
going to his job to tell him just what I'm thinking!

I decide to take an early lunch and run the five blocks to
Rick's office in the Mutual Benefits building before he left
to take lunch himself. I arrive at the reception desk and the
security person manning the desk points out at the door
behind him signaling to me that I just missed Rick leaving
out the revolving door in the back of the building. So I hurry
past reception at out the other entrance.

"Rick! Rick!" I yell towards his back. I took mental notice that Rick acknowledges that I'm in his presence by turning around with a hard scowl and look of disgust on his face.

"What is it Shugar? I'm on my way out to grab lunch" he states with a slight air of arrogance in his voice.

"I've been calling and leaving you messages for the last couple of days Rick? And you haven't returned any of my calls. Your daughter needs ballet shoes for her dance class and you need to pay for that dance class as we agreed. And besides that, I miss you."

"I need to pay for it? Shugar. I just bought a brand new car and moved into the condo, not to mention I have my student loans to start paying off. Why can't you pay for it or ask my Dad for the money like you been doing?" Rick replies in a very irritated whisper so as not to make a scene in the lobby.

I lean into Rick's voice with my hands on my hip and say, "Are you serious? You know…ever since you started this little job you been acting funny. You don't return my calls, you barely invite me over to spend time with you lately and now you don't want to help with your daughter like you promised you would do the minute you graduated college and found a job. And don't let me speak on Miss Thang; your "friend. You need to be the man you said you was gonna be and take care of your family; me and Stormy."

"Oh now I'm not a man? I'm not a man Shugar? I'm not a man because I moved out my parent's house, graduated college, bought a car and a condo and by the way, I am paying child support now." Rick snaps back.

"Rick. You drop off a measly $100 bucks every week to

23

my mom for keeping Stormy every afternoon and evening after daycare so WE can go to work and you call THAT paying me child support? Negro please! I've been taking care of that little girls since she was born by myself while you went away to college remember? And thank God for your parents and my mother for stepping up and stepping in where you couldn't Mr. Man. Being a single parent has not been a cake walk and if I didn't…."

"If you didn't what? If you didn't what Shugar? Have that money from the settlement you received from the crime victim's fund? What was it…$15-20 thousand dollars you got 3 years ago? You wasn't the only one who was a victim Shugar! I was too. And you didn't offer me two fucking cents of that damn money. Then I find out from my parents that you and your family went ahead and freaked that little bit of money and made a small fortune off it from some small investments and still didn't tell me nothing about that shit. So yeah. You got the money to take care Stormy by yourself so do it and stop looking for my help like I'm her real father or something?"

"What did you just say?" I ask with absolute astonishment in my voice. My hands begin quaking as my mind is racing to make sense of what Rick just said. Did he just say he is NOT Stormy's father?

"Are you trying to say you're not her father Rick?"

"C'mon Shugar. She don't look nothing like me. Her complexion so light, she look almost white. I'm black as hell. She got two different colored eyes. I have two brown eyes. And where she get reddish brown hair and them big round eyes from Shugar? You are as dark as I am with chinky eyes and she don't look like either one of us at all.

24

Nowhere. Shit. To be honest she look like one of ... Never mind." Rick sighs and takes a deep breath. He pauses for a moment and realizes the mistake he just made.

He looks me in my face and sees the hurt he is causing me and puts both hands on my shoulders and pulls me into to his body where I begin to weep into his chest. How could he say that? How could he think that?

Ricks pulls into the closed in waiting area of the lobby and talks into the top of head, "You know Shugar? I'm stressed out about all these new bills and moving and stuff and I'm taking it out on you. I'm sorry. But you're right. I should help you out with OUR daughter and now that I'm working, I will. Promise. I will take my little pumpkin to get her shoes and spend some time with her this weekend. In fact, I'll come by tonight to pick her up and keep her all weekend so you can go do you with your girlfriends." He steps back enough to pull my face up to his. "I'm sorry Shugar. I shouldn't have said that. That gorgeous little creature we created is all mines and I know it. Please forgive me?"

I shake my head yes at Rick and he pecks me on the lips and gently guides me back around to the front of his building and tells me he will call me after work when he arrives home. There isn't anything he can say to fix my heart that just broke into a thousand pieces so I fake a faint smile, wave good bye and head back to my own office. Once I arrive back at my desk, I pretend to have eaten something during lunch that doesn't agree with me and tell my manager I need to go home because I feel sick. When I do get home, I go to my room, shut the door and cry myself to sleep.

Six hours have past and I feel my little angel face

stirring in her sleep under me, I wouldn't have awakened at 7 pm from my heartbroken slumber if I didn't know she was there with me in my bedroom. My mother must have laid her down with me after day care.

I stare down and that face and appreciate just how exceptionally beautiful Stormy is for a small child. And as I study her features I recognize my mother's nose and my ears in her features. I see the resemblance in her to Rick too, why can't he?

I hear a horn blowing outside the window as my Mom is yelling up the stairs to me that Rick's mom is outside waiting to pick up Stormy.

I'm thinking, what? I thought Rick said he was coming by to pick her up. This is crazy. Let me call him to see what is going on.

"Rick. Why didn't you come yourself to pick up the baby?"........... "You're that busy that you had your mother do it or are you trying to avoid me?" ...... "So, do you at least want me to come over later to watch a movie with you two or something?"..... "Oh. Ok. Well, I'll pack her favorite blanket too; otherwise she'll get super cranky from that long ride to the Poconos without it and I'll send her humidifier just in case the air up there bothers her at night."...... . "Well alright Rick. Take care of my baby and call me as soon as you are all back. I love y...." CLICK

I can only stare at the phone in my hand. I'm not sure how to react to that brief conversation. I don't know what to make of Rick lately at all.

I'm entering the living room and overhear my mother and Ethan discussing the fact that Rick's parents picked up the baby, not Rick himself and that something must have happened earlier between him and I because I apparently came home and cried myself to sleep. Wow! That are sitting right here talking about me like my bedroom isn't an earshot away.

"You want to know something Ethan?" my mother asks my brother as he is checking his duffle bag once more time to ensure he has packed everything he'll need for his trip back home to Atlanta.

"That boy don't give a damn about Shugar but you can't tell that girl his shit don't stink. All the time running her mouth about how they gonna be married and live happily ever after. Shit. She'd be lucky he offer her a friendship ring, never mind an engagement ring. And Lord knows I've always tried to get her to understand that no man wants damaged goods no anyway."

"Mom!" Ethan stares into our mother's face with disbelief.

"Why would you say Shugar is damaged goods? What happened to her is not her fault and you of all people should know that it don't make her damaged. I mean, look at all that girl has done for herself. She could have gone crazy after that incident but she didn't. Shugar is a strong person to deal with that memory and still be able to look Rick in his face. I don't know if I could do it."

I love my brother for always having my back.

"Here you go Ethan!" Now my mom is heated that my brother checked her... again.

"I don't mean that Shugar is damaged but honestly, but everybody know what happened to her and I don't know anybody that wants to deal with that much baggage. Hell, she found out she was pregnant three weeks following that,

that, that.. Well, you know what I'm talking about, and once she found out she was pregnant, most people assumed that she was pregnant by.... You know. Regardless of her being with child, it's like she ignored those boys did that to her and was unfaltering in believing having Stormy was the best thing in the world that could have happened to her. And when the doctors and therapists all suggested she abort the pregnancy, not sure who the father was, that girl became enraged and changed her personality altogether. But see. I know the truth. I know what she about and she ain't fooling anybody. Sure, she pulled herself together and she is a good mother to Stormy but Shugar is nobody's saint and there is no point in pretending she is. She stay hanging out with that Sincere character and Bilal still sniffing around her ass as well. But it's that young boy Ibin from across the street that got me wondering what he looking for from Shugar."

"Mother." Ethan says. Totally tired of the conversation already, he finishes.

"Shugar has been through a lot and as far as I'm concerned she is fine and so is my niece. As for Rick, he should be kissing Shugar's ass every day we didn't kill him when all that shit went down. Regardless, if you that concerned with your daughter's well-being you would be talking to her and not about her to me. It is crazy that the two of you never discussed this situation. Ever. Your daughter still needs you Mom. Anyway, I gotta get on the road. Tell everybody I said good bye and I'll call Shugar later to check on her. Love you."

As Ethan was throwing his bag over his shoulder, I crept back up the stairs, into my room and packed my own overnight bag. No way was I staying in this space with all this negative energy around me after hearing all that. Besides, Stormy was gone for the weekend and I could have some quiet time to myself to figure out what to do about Rick. I'll get a room at the Hilton downtown and stay there tonight.

Just as I slam my truck closed with my overnight bag inside, Ibin startles me walking towards me from the front of the car.

"Where you going gorgeous?" he says in a voice I detect as sad.

"Out." I dryly reply.

"You look like you gonna stay the night out somewhere. You going to your boy's house; the punk?"

I don't know what happened in that moment but I stood there in Ibin's face and broke down.

I mean, I started tearing and wiping my eyes and all of a sudden I couldn't help the noise that was coming from my throat. I had an urge to empty myself of this heaviness I was feeling right there at the trunk of my car with Ibin of all people witnessing it.

Barely able to stand, I turned and leaned my behind on the bumper, hunkered my head into my knees and I cried. I think I had been crying for at least five minutes when I realized that Ibin was just staring at me with a look on his face that said he felt sorry for me. That look in his face was a trigger and I stopped the heaving, eye wiping, sniffling and pulled myself together as quickly as I could. I don't ever want anyone to feel sorry for me; I'm not a victim. I am not a fucking victim!

"I'm good. Excuse me Ibin. I have to go." I say as I

pushed him aside and tried to open my door. But he rushed over and leaned his muscular body against the frame of the door to keep me from climbing in.

"Shugar. Relax. I'm not trying to hurt you or anything but you look like shit and you obviously dealing with something. Slow down Ma. Breathe before you pull off. I wasn't trying to start nothing with you this time." He had a look of concern in his eyes now. I couldn't deny that.

I took a deep breathe but have no intentions of saying anything until he gets out of my way and allows me to leave.

"You alright now? Shugar? Oh. You on your tough girl shit...... " Ibin is growing increasingly annoyed with my attitude towards him and I can't afford to make what feels like another enemy.

"Yeah. I said I'm okay. I just need to get away from this house. Too much hateful energy and I need a break from this whole neighborhood", I say as I look into his eyes for the first time.

"Where you going?" he asks me again.

"Downtown to the Hilton for the night. Maybe two. My friend works there and hooks me up with a room from time to time...when I need to clear my head."

"You want some company?" Ibin wonders out loud.

"Company?" I ask him back.

Just how does he find the nerve to ask me a question like that? I thought I made it understood that he and I are not cool like that and we won't ever be.

"I don't mean company, company. I mean just someone to chill with. Have a glass of wine with. Relax. Talk. I'm not trying to insinuate anything else. Honest", he chuckles.

I think about his proposal for a few seconds. I really hate being alone and he standing here. Fuck it.

"Okay."

"Okay? You sure?" Ibin is surprised by my answer.

"Yeah. Okay. You can come but we are not fucking, sucking or licking…nothing like that. I am not a whore who gets down like that."

"Whoa Shugar… I didn't say anything about that. I know you don't get down like that. Chill out", he insists.

We check into the Junior Suite of the hotel and it is nice. I immediately remove the bottle of Merlot from my overnight bag and poor myself a much needed glass as Ibin removes a small bottle of Hennessy from his back pocket and takes his own sip. We both take a few moments to walk around the room and check out the amenities and observe the wet bar.

Finally, we decide to sit on the loveseat provided and inhale the silence of the room. I start to relax and appreciate the time I offered myself to get away from my mother and her pessimism.

Ibin and I begin to talk about random things regarding the neighborhood and the players in it. We sip wine and cognac and become more and more tranquil as the late evening became the wee hours of the morning. At one point, he removed himself to the bathroom where he smoked a very green aromatic blunt and re-joined me in the room now even more relaxed. It was nice to just talk to someone about nothing and feel content with them at the same time.

"So, when my Dad died, my mom turned to drugs to deal with his death and I was too young really to do anything about it." His voice trails off as he stares emptily at the ceiling as he was sitting in a chair across from the bed I was laying in fully clothed.

An hour or so of more conversation and I finally excuse myself to the bathroom and change into a pair of sweat pants and oversized t-shirt to get more comfortable. I re-enter the sleeping area to find that Ibin had neatly placed his Timberland boots by the door and folded his jeans and white t-shirt in the desk chair. He was left in a pair of blue basketball shorts and a very fitted wife-beater t-shirt. Geesh!

I didn't make mention of his more comfortable attire and he didn't mention mine in return but he had poured me another glass of wine and offered me a bite of his apple that he cleverly hid in his hoodie jacket.

"So what's your story Shugar? Tell me about yourself; something you haven't told another living soul." He chuckled, not knowing how serious this conversation was about to get.

Until this moment, no one had asked me to tell them anything about me that they had a real interest in so I pondered that question and decided, here was my chance to see what he was made of. I started talking. Revealing my own truth.

"When I was nineteen years old I was raped. Not just raped either. I was violently bruised, battered and broken by seven different men who sodomized me with sticks, soda cans and their bare fists. It all started one night when I was walking with my then-boyfriend, Rick......"

In the darkness of the hotel room and without interruption or hesitation on either of our parts, I told Ibin every wretched detail of the day that changed my life forever. I told him about how different the relationship with

my mother had become and how filtered the bonds with my
brothers and sister are since that incident. I dumped every
fragmented piece of my heart at his lap and when I was done
talking, I quietly waited for him to tell me it was too heavy
to bare and leave me to deal like everyone before him had.
It's what I had become use to except I had never gotten
through the entire story with anyone before now because no
one appeared strong enough to handle hearing it.

After no reply from Ibin at all, I decided to roll over and
look into his face to at least see his reaction since he clearly
had no words to share. When he noticed me looking, he
wiped tears from his eyes and pulled me close under his
arms. He and I stayed closed to one another for a long while
allowing the last glass of wine to take its course. Eventually
I grow so tired I can barely keep my eyes open any longer
and I curl up under next to his body and ultimately fall
asleep.

Later, I jump out of my sleep and sit straight up in the
bed holding my chest and trying to control my heavy
breathing. I forget where I am as I feel Ibin grab my hand
and sits up alongside me. But it takes me a few seconds to
focus on his face and understand what the hell was going on.
I couldn't decide immediately if I was chased into this room
or did Ibin pull me in here or did they drag me into this
darkness. I'm unmoving in that pose; fearful to even blink.

"Shugar? You okay?" Ibin is talking softly as he puts his
hands around my shoulders. I stiffen myself even more.
"It's me Shugar… Shugar. It's me. Ibin."

I blink once. I blink again and turn my head slowly and
take in the darkness of the room and do my best to slow the
racing of my brain. I close my eyes really tight and inhale.

Exhale. Inhale. Exhale. Innnhaallee. Exxxhalllee. Okay.......
I open my eyes again and look into Ibin's face.

"You okay?", he asks again. I shake my head yes and
wipe the lone tear racing down my face.

Ibin pulls me into his chest and my head ends up under
his chin as he wraps his arms around my body and we lay
down again slowly. Carefully, he rubs and pats my back like
a mother would a small child. My body was beginning to
lose its rigidness and I began to calm down a little more and
sleepiness was returning to my state of being. I was thinking
they weren't gonna find me here so I can go back to sleep. I
knew I was safe where I was and it's where I wanted to
stay....for now anyway.

With a kiss to the forehead, as I'm fighting the drift to a
more inviting place in my mind, I heard Ibin say, "I got you
Shugar. Ain't nobody gonna hurt you no more. Shhh. I got
you."

4 JOURNAL ENTRY
August 30, 1997

It's Stormy's birthday today and I couldn't be more thrilled to see the look on her face when Rick brings her to the hall from being with him the last four weeks of summer and she sees the big party Jamil, Jamal and my mom planned for her. She is going to be so excited about it.

The princess themed event is definitely over the top for an seven-year-old but they all insisted on spending that kind of money and I was basically overruled. Custom styled Barbie cupcakes designed to have the actual cupcake be the ball gown of those miniature dolls was such a cool idea. That along with the lavish decorations and whimsical clowns and elaborate balloon bouquets are simply gorgeous. Stormy is a lucky little girl to have her uncles' think so much of her to do this. None-the-less, my little angel is going to be so surprised to see all of her classmates and cousins here.

It's going to be strange though to be in the same room with Rick for more than ten minutes. It is his daughter's birthday party and everyone would expect him to be here I suppose. But if he brings his side-bitch I will be heated. Trina has no business anywhere around me and my daughter and especially not during our "family time". Rick knows how I feel about that and he better respect it.

"MOMMY!" Stormy screams at me as she burst through the doors of the event hall's foyer, running as fast as she can to me. "Oh my angel." I say to her as I scoop her up in my arms. It feels so good to hold this little miracle again. I've missed her terribly.

"How is Mommy's angel?" I ask her as I stoop to put her down and stand on my knees to be closer to her height. "Let me look at you." I say. I take her soft hand in mine and twirl her around as if she was a display mannequin. "You are looking fabulous Sweetheart and look at those sneakers. Are they lighting up every time you take a step?" I ask her in my I've-missed-you-so-much-I-have-to-talk-super-sweet voice.

"Yes Mommy! They light up. Look!" Stormy says as she takes off around the little space outside her party, stomping her very pink My Little Pony sneakers on the ground to show me how they work. Her neon colored tutu matches the jean jacket she has on and the ruffle fold down socks add the right amount of innocence to the overall look of her birthday outfit.

As my daughter is flying around the room, now amusing herself with the lights, I shoot Rick a very dirty look as if we were alone; I want to kill him for this bullshit he just pulled.

"That is beautiful Dollface!" I yell at Stormy to get her attention. She comes running back up to me and halts directly on top of my feet, looks up at me and quietly says, "Mommy, whose having a party today?"

Together Rick and I say, "YOU!!" And we open the door to all her guests yelling "SURPRISE!!!!!"

Stormy didn't know where to look first. But she saw my

mom standing up front with Uncle Ethan and she bolted right to them and offered up a big hug. Then she saw her Pop-Pop and Nanny, Rick's parents, and they kissed and hugged all over their only grandchild. She was so happy. Stormy turned around and looked back at Rick and I standing in the doorway and she pranced right over and put her hands in both of ours as she ushered us in to her party like she was her own hostess; everyone was clapping and cheering her on. I leaned down and moved that massive mound of hair away from her ear and whispered, "Say thank you everybody."

And she did to another roar of claps and cheers. Jamal cued the DJ to start the music and dancing ensued immediately on the dance floor.

I caught my sister Kyra's eye from the corner where she was standing with her boyfriend and without words, told her to keep a watch on my baby while I dealt with Rick. She nodded back in a manner I knew she understood.

"Rick I need to speak to you outside please." I say with such annoyance, I'm almost daring him to not comply.

"Here we go." He says as we both turn and head out towards the parking lot of the building.

I don't waste two seconds before I start to go in.

"You have the fucking audacity to bring your bitch to my baby birthday party and flaunt her around like that shit is okay? What the fuck is wrong with you Rick? You can't have more respect for me and your daughter than to not embarrass us at her birthday party? And I know you didn't let that trick do my baby's hair like that; looking like a wild baby lion or something. Her hair looks crazy, flying all around like that. When I sent her off to you, it was all braided up with beads that should have lasted just fine for four weeks."

"First of all," he starts. "Stormy is only seven years old and she don't even know what embarrassment means so shut the fuck up with all that. You're the one that's embarrassed because you got people in their thinking you and I are still a couple and you know we broke up damn-near a year ago. If you want to run around here pretending we still together then you deserve to be embarrassed cause I'm not hiding Trina from nobody for your sake. Fuck that."

"Oh, it's like that Rick? Fuck me hunh? Ok. Well, let me explain something to you since you don't seem to understand the rules to a break up. When you call yourself ending one relationship to supposedly be in another one, you stop fucking the first chick and telling her that you still love her, meaning ME!" I'm yelling now and becoming increasingly excited by the moment.

"Shugar! I think you are really delusional girl. For real. We fuck and I tell you I love you. So what. You know what it is… it's just a fuck! Damn! What the hell? You think just because you let me hit that from time-to-time still I'm supposed stay in a relationship with you? NO! That ain't how this works. And as far as Stormy's hair is concerned, Trina took her hair loose from them loud stupid beads two weeks ago. She and her girlfriend took her to New York to a modeling agency and nobody is going to take my daughter seriously if she wearing that ghetto hairstyle. So Trina took Stormy to her hairdresser and had them make her hair straight or whatever. You need to be thanking my girl for that." Rick is rambling on and on.

"Yo Shugar. Is there a problem?." Rick and I both look

down in lust at this pretty ass black-on-black, shiny 1998 BMW 740il. Gorgeous! It was Ibin. He's driving and Jamil was riding shotgun in the passenger seat, both windows down trying to make since of the scene Rick and I are creating.

Jamil looks like he is as high as a kite right now as he hurdles from the passenger door and practically jumps over the hood of the car. "Rick. Are you having a problem with my sister right now Bruh?"

"Naw. It ain't a problem Jamil." Rick struggles to explain. "I was just clearing up to your sister about how my girl took our daughter to the City and had her take some flicks for a modeling agency, Man. Your niece gonna be a star one day…" His voice is very shaky and nervous.

"Well do yourself a favor Bruh. Take about three steps back outta Shugar's face and talk like a man to my sister my dude. You looking a little aggressive right now and my sister ain't looking too comfortable with yall's conversation." Jamil finishes.

By now, Ibin has parked his car, locked it and is working his way towards our gathering in a hurry. I don't think I've ever seen him so put together before now. The jeans are the right amount of too big and the crisp new beef and broccoli Timbs paired with the white wife beater tank top piped out by brown leather is hitting. I'm thinking that he looks damn good.

"You aight Shugar?" Ibin asks as he approaches us. He walks right up to Rick's face and says to me, "Cause you look upset. You upset about something?"

Rick is not appreciating having his manhood tested right here in an open parking lot at all. He takes a step back himself and squares up to Ibin as he looks him up and down.

"Shugar and I are discussing business pertaining to OUR daughter if you don't mind. And if she looks any kind of uncomfortable, it don't have anything to do with you. I can take care of my woman." Rick says with a puffed up chest.

Ibin peers down at me and I'm grinning a school-girl's grin at Rick because he calls me "his woman". I'm loving that he is claiming me again and for that reason I thought it a good idea to end this confrontation before it even gets started.

"Jamil and Ibin, I am alright. We was just disagreeing over Stormy's birthday gift from us. I let Rick pick it out and of course he goes over the top and buys her this huge motorized car that I think it's just too much and well... you know. We got into it a little bit but everything is good." I tried my best to make that sound good.

Jamil seems content with my answer but Ibin isn't the least bit convinced but for my sake he backs down.

"Aight", he says still staring into Rick's face with hands clenched tight at this sides.

I stand between the two men and shove Ibin back a bit to put some space and less opportunity between the two.

"Well, go 'head inside and join the party guys. Stormy is going to be very excited to see you Uncle Jamil." I'm laughing it off as best I could, trying to lighten the mood in this space.

Jamil taps Ibin on his shoulder and signals for him to relax and follow him inside the event hall. And although Ibin concedes, he doesn't appear to have calmed down much since Rick stood up to him.

"Aight Shugg. I'ma see you inside." Ibin says and walks off not taking his eyes off Rick.

Immediately after Jamil and Ibin make it across the parking lot and into the event hall, Rick begins to tear into me.

"Who the fuck is this dude Shugar? Fuck! He always seems to be around and he always seems to be fucking ice-grilling me for some strange reason. You know this guy?" Rick is talking so loud I'm afraid the twosome, Jamil and Ibin, will come back out.

"Lower your voice Rick!" I hiss at him. "All this damn yelling is causing a scene out here...... That's Jamil's friend Ibin. You've seen him around before and please know that's just Jamil's road dog that's all Baby." I'm trying my hardest to put a little sugar in my voice to make this situation work in my favor with Rick.

"I don't give a fuck who he is but he better stay outta my face before he catch a hot one to his mouth!" Rick is heated.

"And back to what I was saying anyway. Look. I'ma stop fucking around with you and shit cause I see you don't know how to separate sex from being in a relationship. Besides, this thing with Trina is getting serious and I don't want to fuck that up by still dipping back and forth with you."

Now I'm pissed. Didn't he just call me his woman two seconds ago? Isn't he the one always paging me and leaving me messages about wanting to make love to me again and how he misses my kisses and what-have-you? And wasn't it just like a month and a half ago that he was telling me how sexy I was as he was tracing the scars on my breasts and thighs while I was naked, laid up the on the floor of the bedroom next to the fireplace? Now he wants to act like none of that meant anything to him or that I'm not relevant anymore.

"Wow Rick. I thought you and I was really working on being back together and everything and you say that to me? I mean… You said the only reason why we broke up to begin with was so you could take some time to explore being on your own a little bit cause we had been going non-stop for like eight years. And you said, I needed to make sure you are who I wanted too. I believed that shit Rick and I thought I made it clear that I didn't want to be with anybody else." I step closer to Rick and braised my breasts across his chest. I want him to know I still feel the same about him. I still love him.

"Shugar." He says calmly as he takes my hands in his. "It's over Baby. I can't do this anymore with you. You deserve to be with somebody that feels that same way about you. It ain't me no more. I think we out grew each other and I'm sorry. I'ma be with Trina exclusively and try to make that work okay? "

I'm crushed. "It's not okay Rick."

I feel like I need to beg him to not leave me but I can't bring myself to go that low.

"I've loved you since I was eighteen years old Rick and look what we've been through together and I'm still here." I'm holding on to his hands for dear life. "What can I do to make you stay Rick? Hunh? You want me to lose some more weight? Grow my hair out longer? Or get plastic surgery to have the scars removed? Rick? What do you want me to do? I'll do it. I swear Rick. I'll do whatever you want me to do."

But I am begging.

I'm pleading for what feels like my life at this moment and if I can't convince Rick to stay with me it will mean that I have to change. I will have to change ME and exist without Rick being what I thought was my rock. How in the hell do I do that without him. Who is going to love me like Rick did? Who?

"And what about Stormy Rick? She needs you be in her life. She is not supposed to grow up without her Daddy."

Rick face says he feels sorry for me and that bothers me. It bothers me a lot. Through my tears I decided at that moment to pull myself together and stop groveling to him. If he don't want me oh well! It will be his lost; not mine. I don't ever want anyone to feel sorry for me. I am not a victim.

"I'ma always be in Stormy's life..." he attempts to finish a sentence but I cut him off.

"You know what Rick? If you don't want to be with me anymore FINE! But don't be making any booty calls to be either. And don't be calling asking me to borrow money or to run errands for you. And since you wanna make whatever you got going on with Trina work, don't you ask me ever again to do a fuckin' threesome with you and her no fuckin' more. As far as Stormy is concerned, you will absolutely be her father; that's for damn sure. And you will pay me child-support. On time. No excuses." I look Rick up and down and ignore the surprised look on his face.

"Bye Rick. You can go and enjoy your daughter's birthday party now." Without so much as a peep, Rick turns around and walks away.

To be honest, he looked relieved to be finally rid of me.

But I feel like shit at that moment. It is beginning to seep into my heart that Rick and I was no more and that thought was causing all kinds of turmoil in my gut at that instant. I feel sick like I need to throw up so I run towards the big green garbage dumpster in the corner of the parking lot and earl my lunch.

As I wipe my mouth and find a tissue in the pocket of my dress pants to clean my face, I look up to see Ibin handing me more tissue.

"You ain't need that niggah anyway. Fuck him. You got me." Was Ibin's only words as he walked me back to the building where my daughter was inside having the time of her young life. I smiled at that thought and found my way back to the party.

Rick is standing near the bar with a drink in hand cuddling up to Trina as she giggles and grins back at him. My daughter is standing in the middle of a circle, dancing and laughing with her Pop-Pop while my brothers, sister and mother and cheering her on. "Go Stormy! Go Stormy! Go Stormy!"

Watching her smile like that lifts my burdens suddenly and for a short while, I'm so elated I have this little life to sustain me for now and keep my mind off her trifling father. But out of the corner of my eye I notice a young lady who arrived with my sister Kyra approach Ibin. She takes his hands in hers and ushers him to the corner near the coat-check room. Then she whispers something to him and he grins and she grins back. And I can't turn my head away as they start to kiss. I can tell he enjoys it and I go back to crushed.

5 JOURNAL ENTRY
November 27, 1997

My mother has again assigned me the lowest job possible in preparing the Thanksgiving meal; cutting up the vegetables to be used in the stuffing and other dishes. Everyone knows how much I think this job sucks. I mean, she's taken time out to teach my younger sister, Kyra how to cook southern style foods and clearly at some point she took the same time with all three of my brothers over the years. But I've never graduated past chopping and cleaning where my mother's teachings are concerned and it bothers me that I know she knows that. Whatever. I'll get over it. I can get around well enough in the kitchen just from my observances of my her style and the rest, I guess I'll just learn from trial and error.

The house is full of energy with my siblings, aunties, cousins and uncles all arriving throughout the day. And I love this time of year; when it's about the family. My brother Ethan will be here with his wife and kids. So will my favorite cousin Na-Na and her girlfriend that, in spite of them being gay, everybody just loves them as a couple. But no family gathering is complete without my loud and brash

Uncle James who says what is exactly on his mind and don't care who gets hurt in the cross fire. It's just how he's always been. You gotta love him though.

"Hey Girl", my Uncle James is yelling at me from across the living room. "Bring me a beer out yo momma's fridge and that bowl of nuts off the buffet. Shit! I'm hungry and Sheila gone be cooking to the last damn minute." I humbly do as I'm told and pass him the items he so rudely asked for and on cue he says, "You show growed up to be a pretty little thing over there Shugar. You still with that lousy ass Rick boy?"

"No Uncle James. Rick and I broke up a few months back. Can I get you anything else while I'm up though?"

"Well it's about damn time cause that boy was a pussy and everybody knew it but your silly ass. What took you so damn long to figure it out?" He is still questioning me and I'm feeling real uncomfortable.

"Nothing Uncle James. I'm good. I mean… Rick and I are good. It was just time to go our separate ways is all." I'm gritting me teeth and staring at him square in his eyes to shut him down hopefully but that doesn't work either.

"Ever since them boys jumped all over you, I told yo momma that that Rick boy wasn't gonna be around much longer in no relationship with you. No way no man gonna stay with no woman they look at as, as, … you know,…… messed up. I don't mean tampered with but more like scarred emotionally. Cause how can a man deal with that? Right? But then Sheila and everybody say you came through just fine and act like it don't bother you or nothing and you running around here taking care of that baby yours like she the best thing since slice bread."

46

Now I'm gonna cut him off. I hate these kinds of conversations when they seem to be only about me and what happened to me all those years ago. I mean. It's over. And it pisses me off that no one speaks on it for years at a time but when they do, it's in a gossiping manner like I'm some fictional character or something. I mean, damn.

"Okay Uncle James. Rick is still my daughter's father and in spite of how you or anybody else feel towards him, I ask that you at the very least, respect Stormy and not speak ill about her dad in earshot of her hearing it. And as far as Rick being a pussy; that's your opinion and you need to keep it too yourself. Thank you very much."

But my mother chimes in from the kitchen, "Alright now Shugar. Don't be getting fresh with your Uncle. I don't care how old you are. You understand me little girl? James can say whatever he want to say in here. This is my damn house and…" Her bullshit gets interrupted by the doorbell.

Without hesitation, I turn my back to my mother and Uncle and hurry through the mud room and snatch open the door to invite whoever was on the other side to come in and join the madness that was about to ensue.

To my surprise, it's a very tall white man, wearing a black and white jersey, jeans a badge around his neck asking for Jamil as if they were old friends.

I stare at him with a uncertain look on my face and ask if anything is wrong and cheerfully he says, "Nope Shugar. Nothing is wrong. Just need to speak to my man. Can you go get 'em for me please?"

First. How the hell does he know my name and second, why is the white cop at my house on Thanksgiving day looking for my brother? This is some bullshit.

"Jamil. Door for you!" I yell with my back turned to the still opened door.

But Jamaal arrives first and asks, "Who is it?"

"Some white guy. I think he a cop", I say to Jamaal who is obviously going to pose as his brother at this moment as he opens the door enough to let himself outside on the porch. But I step outside too so I can understand what this is about myself. After all, these are my brothers and I know it got something to do with some street shit and I want to know what.

"Can I help you?" Jamaal is standing firm with his hands stuffed in the pockets of his jeans calmly and offering not much more of a gesture to this person. But I notice a black Ford crown vic car blocking the driveway and two passengers in the car. One in the passenger side and one in the back seat. Both wearing these same badges around their necks. Now I'm a little concerned.

"You're not Jamil, Jamaal." This white guy starts laughing and looking back to his partners in the car, pointing at Jamaal and me standing in the doorway.

"Shugar? I did say Jamil didn't I? Yeah. I think I did. I did clearly say Jamil. Not his brother Jamaal. But it doesn't matter cause Jamil will get this message regardless.

"And what message is that partner?" Jamal states firmly, not taking his eyes of this guy standing on my porch attempting to make a mockery out of us in this moment.

The door is pulled open from the inside and out walks my oldest brother Ethan standing larger than life wanting to make since of who was at the door and what was taking his younger brother and sister so long to resolve.

"Is there a problem....Officer?" Ethan interjected as he

took a step onto the porch.

"Actually Private Ethan Brown, there isn't a problem at all. I was just telling your brother here and your gorgeous sister, that I was just stopping by on this fine evening to say hello to your other brother Jamil but since he isn't home I'd like you to deliver a message to him and his friend Ibin for me if you'd please?"

"And what's that Officer?"

"No. It's Agent Brentwell of the Federal Bureau of Investigations Narcotics Unit. And you tell your brother Jamil that the time has come to do the right thing. Tell him he has two hours to either talk to us about Carlyle or his entire squad is going down."

"Is that right Agent Brentwell?" It was taking everything my brother had to stay calm but I can tell he wanted to grab this guy by his neck and squeeze until his finger laced into each other.

"That's exactly right Private Brown." And with that the white guy exited our porch, walked back down to his waiting partner, climbed into the driver's seat and drove off.

As soon as the door shut and the three of us were back inside standing in the foyer, Ethan grimaced at us and began his big-brother-lecture.

"Whatever Jamil is doing out there in those streets had better not find its way in Mommy's house. Now you two can stand here and pretend you don't know what that was all about but I know you know the whole truth. And somebody had better do some thinking and help Jamil find his way out of this mess cause him and that Ibin, don't know how to do anything except spend money and get high all damn day. Let me remind you that Mommy can lose this house and all her possessions because of some shit your brother got himself into and when I leave here to go back home, it will be up to you two to make sure Mommy and Kyra don't get hurt not to mention Stormy. You understand?"

I let out a frustrated sigh. As normal, Ethan was being overly dramatic. Jamil is selling drugs but I doubt it's to the extent of that little show they just put on. "Aight Ethan. God. Relax. I will talk to Jamil after everyone leaves later on and find out what is going on and make sure he ain't doing anything to get any of us in any kind of trouble. Okay?"

"Shugar. You worry about Stormy and Jamal and I will talk to Jamil later. I heard about his little operation and his cronies he call soldiers out there and from my understanding he pulling in a lot of dough. Fine. If he wants to throw away his life and take them boys down with him, that's his business. But what he not gonna do is anything that puts my family in any kind of danger. I will break his ass before I let that happen."

Ethan was so mad he went straight to the basement and left Jamal and I just standing there. I looked over at my brother and he shrugged his shoulders, shook his head and we rejoined the rest of the family in the dining room where a loud game of spades had begun.

Ibin and I are taking turns exchanging glances in the basement while we both pretended to be engrossed in the football game that everyone else was watching on the television. I had observed him and Jamil come in a while earlier and I can tell by the worried look on Jamil's face that Ethan had already spoken to him about the FBI coming by prior.

50

As the evening wore on to the early hours of the next morning, I eventually decided it was time to take myself up to bed. I began saying my goodnights to the remaining guests and was heading towards the basement stairs.

"Yo. Shugar. Can I talk to you for second?" Ibin looked tired himself but I can tell he had been waiting for this moment most of the evening. He followed me up to the empty first floor and to the bottom of the stairs leading to my bedroom.

He was standing so tall over me. Broad shoulders and rugged. I can smell his cologne that was lingering in the air. Fahrenheit. My favorite.

"What's up Ibin?" I was tired and wasn't really up for conversation so late or rather early in the morning. I had been helping my mother all day with cooking and cleaning up after what felt like hundreds and hundreds of guests. Thank goodness Stormy was spending the remainder of this holiday weekend with her other family because that meant I could sleep late.

"Shugar." Ibin mumbled. He kept his eyes lowered, keeping it gangsta he thought, struggling to conceal his like for me.

"I haven't really seen you around the last couple of months. You know....not since your daughter's birthday party this past summer. How you been?"

"Yea I know. I've seen you though. You and Jamil look like you are on the come up out there. But you two better be careful cause those agents that came by today don't sound like they playing."

"Whatever! They don't have shit on me and your brother and we ain't turning informant on Carlyle so they can just ride with that bullshit. That ain't what we about." He seemed annoyed with the thought.

"Well, whatever you are doing out there, I hope you all have a handle on it cause I don't want to see anybody get hurt. I heard that they picked up Carlyle's girlfriend, Brooklyn, this morning on some wire-tap confessions."

"Listen. I don't want to talk about no street shit with you Shugar. I just want to know how you been. How you been getting along since you and ole boy broke up? You aight?" He pulls out a cigarette to light up and I give him the look like, 'don't even.' And he smiles at me sheepishly and puts it away nervously.

"I've been good. Getting along. But why you looking at me like that Ibin?" I was initially determined to not flirt with Ibin knowing he had a girlfriend now.

"What?" He couldn't help it. A deep smile crept across his face. Ibin put his head down again, blushing as he reached for the same cigarette. After realizing he couldn't smoke, he let out a, "Humph,"

"Fuck it. I'ma just tell you Shugar."

"Tell me what?"

"Damn! I can't believe I'ma bout to say this shit to you… finally."

"Okay what?" Now I'm just curious to hear it; whatever it is.

"I like you Shugar." He brings his face up to meet my eyes and his look turns serious. "Naw. I'm in love with you. I've been in love with you since the first day I saw you."

"You like me? Are you serious?" I knew he liked me but he said he loved me and I'm astonished. Really at a loss for words but I want to hear it again.

"No. I said that I love you."

"Hunh? You love me? You don't love me Ibin. You may have a little crush on me or something but you don't love me. Do you know what it means to love somebody?" I mean, what else am I going to say in this moment, right?

"Not really but I know what I feel and it's almost like how I love my mother but it's different than that. It's crazy how I got feelings for you like that and you barely know I'm alive. But I do. I love you. And I don't even know why I'm telling you this now but when I saw you today I just felt like I couldn't hold it in anymore. .... I'm not tryna be your man or anything cause I know you not feeling me like that ...." His voice trailed off and he cast his eyes down again and began to fumble with his pockets. He clearly needed a nicotine fix to get him through this. I thought his insecurity was endearing.

"Why? What is it about me that you think you in love with me?"

Just then, he shot his head up sharply and stepped towards me; I'm struck by his sudden move so I put one hand on the banister and take one step backward up one step to put distance between us.

"See. That's the thing Shugar. It's everything about you. The way you talk, the way you dress. The way I see you be with your daughter. How you help your Mom's. You sexy as fuck and you ain't like other girls I know. You different. You smart. And. And. Your eyes. You have the prettiest eyes."

Ibin felt foolish speaking his heart to me. He was supposed to be thorough. Street. It was obvious though that he felt out of his league. Admittedly, I was flattered, but

Ibin was not my type however I did feel appreciative of the attention.

Moving carefully, Ibin pulled me down the stair and into his chest and he kissed me on the forehead gently. My immediate reaction was to close my eyes; I didn't know what else to do. It felt so genuine to me. It wasn't lustful or sexual at all. No one had ever kissed me on the forehead before Ibin and I'm hoping that's his special thing reserved just for me because it was the second time he had done it since I'd known him. I looked up in his face and he was staring back down at me.

Softly, I glided Ibin against the front door with my chest and pressed up against him. I wanted him to kiss me but he had to make the first move and he did.

First, it was small pecks on the lips and he wrapped his huge hands around my waist so I stepped in even closer. But then the kissing became more and more intense and he slid his tongue in my mouth and I felt a bulge come between us.

We went on like that for at least five minutes before my senses came back to me and I realized what we were doing; and so did he.

"Damn. I'm sorry Shugar. I, I shouldn't have kissed you like that." He took a few steps back but still had his hands around my waist. I wiped my mouth and looked for the courage to look up at him.

"Ummm. You should go." It was all I could think to say.

"Okay." He turned and fumbled at the door knob before he could get a good enough grip to turn it. The door opened and he turned back to look at me. "For real Shugar. I love you." The door shut behind him and I stood there for a few more minutes trying to make sense of why I kissed Ibin. But more importantly, why I liked it.

I didn't even bother to change out of my clothes as I crashed across my bed. I was exhausted and because I promised my friends to go shopping in a couple of hours, there was no point of getting comfortable. Before I drifted off to sleep, I looked out my window towards Ibin's house and saw his bedroom light go off in the distance. Years later, he told me he stared out his window that night at mine too.

When I heard the harsh banging against the door, I originally thought I left the television on in my room and was hearing the remnants of some movie. But as I became more and more awake, the banging was more like a thunderous slam against the front door to the house. And I heard loud yelling and then more rams to the door. I jumped up and ran to the top of the stairs where I met my mother descending down the stairs.

Before she made it the bottom of the last step, the front door flew open and FBI agents flooded our living room, carrying rifles and flashing badges at she and I. We were so confused and scared to death at that moment, we began to scream while staring at each other trying to figure out what was happening.

But then Agent Brentwell stepped out in front and told us he had a warrant to search the house for drugs and guns. He flashed some papers in front of my mother's face and told other agents to check upstairs and the basement.

As they paraded my brother Jamil upstairs from the basement along with my Uncle James, Jamal and two more of their friends, they had me and my mom join them on the living room sofa across from where they had them seated in a row on the floor. They all had their hands behind their backs, held together with some kind of plastic handcuffs. I could only look at my brothers with sympathy in my eyes as we were all wondering what was about to happen to them.

When the agents were done explaining to my mother about the drugs and sawed-off shot guns found in the attic and that they were only going to take Jamil into custody, my mother sat stoic. I asked if I can go to the bathroom after sitting still for the past forty minutes and I was granted permission. So I ran up to the second floor to the master bathroom and grabbed one of the phones as I entered and locked and the door behind me.

I turned on the faucet water to muffle the sound of me talking and dialed my cousin Tammy's house across town to warn her brother that the Feds were at our house and she had better tell Warren to leave. To my surprise, an agent answered the phone and as I started to say hello, I froze at the unfamiliar voice on the other end. There was silence on both lines but I clearly hear commotion going on in the background and then I finally decided to speak.

"Tammy? It's me Shugar..." The voice replied, "Sorry Shugar this is Agent Mercado and there is no point in warning Warren or anybody else in Jamil's crew. We're picking up everybody tonight Darling."

I hung up the phone, turned off the faucet and somberly made my way back down the stairs. As I was entering the living room, the boys were all being ushered out the door to a waiting truck that looked like a huge UPS truck except it was unmarked and white.

As my mom and I stood on the porch, we noticed that in this twilight hour, there were quite a few porch and living room lights on as other guys from my brother's crew were being led out of their houses all around us; being packed into the back of the same truck.

And then I saw him. He was the last one to climb in. His back was hunched and his head was hung low but he looked over at me and I could only stare back at him. My heart sunk. Ibin mouthed to me, "I love you."

They closed the door to the truck and just like that...it was over.

STATE BOARD OF PARDONS
AND PAROLES
Victim Impact Statement

Ms. Brown, the information you provide us today may help this Parole Board better understand how this crime has had an affect by explaining the continuing impact, if any, that it has had on your life as well as the lives of your family members along with any safety concerns that you may hold.

We are obligated to inform you that the impact statement you provide us today will become a permanent part of the Parole Board's case file on the inmate and may be used to determine if this inmate is suitable for parole or should be denied. Because you chose to give a statement at the original sentencing hearing, you are automatically entitled to receive notification of any parole consideration. This has allowed you the opportunity to voice your opinion about the possible parole of the inmate here today.

If you do not have any questions, you may start at any time.

"The word is victim. It's not a word I would use to describe myself but it's the word often used to describe me from age nineteen till now. Before I was raped, I would have described myself as Cherise Shugar Brown. Tall, slender, chocolate brown and attractive with great wits and awesome potential. I woke up that morning knowing that is who I was and although I wasn't quite ready to declare who I was going to become, I still knew I would be an incredible human being. That morning, my mother believed that about me too. In her house, she required that her children be articulate, kind to one another and mannerable. She taught us to dream bigger for ourselves than others would dare dream for us. I met all those requirements and then some and my mother was very proud of me; then.

On that day, October 14, 1990, Cherise Shugar Brown was killed. Left bruised battered and broken in a dirt field where her soul died alone and no one mourned her. There was no funeral or repast where people sat around and reminisced about how she was this wonderful young lady or that she was struck down by seven men in the prime of her life. No one ever connected her name to the word survivor. Her story didn't even make the evening news. Instead, the name Cherise Shugar Brown was replaced with 'rape victim' and the memory of her was buried that night, never to be spoken of again. And what is left of her is ME. SHUGAR.

Because this is a victim impact statement, I must tell you that impact appropriately describes much of my existence since that day. There was the initial impact of fists hitting my face and penises being emptied of their sperm in my mouth and hair. The impact of seven different bodies forcing themselves into mine along with several objects, like broomsticks and pieces of paper bags used as makeshift condoms. Then there were the look of guilt in my brother's eyes as he delivered me to the hospital. My body becoming the source of evidence, my swollen face in the mirror and the look of gut wrenching pain in my mother's eyes as she searched, but never found, the words to comfort her child.

But there was something much deeper. Now, eight years later, I am faced with the task of communicating this impact to you. It is not easily put into words but I will try.

As you can expect, this crime has had a huge impact on

my life. Without this experience, I would have gone on to be whomever Cherise Shugar Brown was destined to be....but instead, today, I am just Shugar. I am a mother of an eight year old daughter who happens to be the center of my life. I have a full-time job that pays well and if I continue on this career path, I could eventually run the firm I work for. I own a nice car and have beautiful clothes and jewelry but none of those things are enough to sustain me.

Because of what these seven men did to me, my mother has never spoken to me or looked at me the same since that day. Instead of expecting me to become a great and accomplished individual, she now only hopes I don't wake her in the middle of the night with my screams from the horrific nightmares. My brothers and sister treat me like I'm made of porcelain; frail and fragile. My friends will introduce me to others with a whispered disclaimer about being a victim of rape. And my boyfriend or rather ex-boyfriend, Rick was never able to get over the fact that he was forced to watch the entire heinous crime and could do nothing to stop it. He stood by me after the fact and told people he was still in a relationship with me but the truth is he checked out of our relationship the instant he left me alone in that lot; he left me when the deed was done. I was broken and he couldn't undo what just happened.

Can you imagine the shame and humiliation he must've felt or still feels? They stripped Rick of his manhood and left him a mere shadow of his old self and I've only been a constant reminder of why he's had to feel this way.

This crime has even impacted the birth of my daughter. She was born in absolute pain with no hope of relief because my insides were so shredded and disfigured, it was a miracle that I could even bore a child, let alone carry her to full term. And I thought having her gave me purpose you know? A different reason to live. A new normal. My daughter is all those things but even her existence, as precious as she is, can't fix me. But what she has become is my new focus however.

As years have passed, I have thought about that day and these men less and less and then more and more. That pattern has remained reliable over the years. And even more consistent is an unrelenting and sometimes severe pain in my stomach. An endless ache in the pit of my belly began in the months following the rape and has been my constant memento that there is an emotion deep inside me that I had still not released. The people I need most have never allowed me to tell them my whole story because it pains THEM so bad.

This past year, my boyfriend and I broke up. My brother was locked away and my mother accidently revealed how she really felt about me being a "victim" of rape. I have no close friends that I spill my guts too and no real connection with anyone to lean on for support during the toughest of times...emotionally. I don't know what genuine love feels like from a man and so I play coy and deflect attention away from me whenever I think anyone is getting too close. Close enough to hurt me. And I was at a moment of breaking completely down when I received a call from Detective Isaac asking if I wanted to participate in this parole board hearing and give an impact statement. I knew almost instantly that my opportunity to heal, to come to terms with the impact on my life this crime has had was right here. Right now.

My intent for participating in this hearing is to begin the

process of closing this chapter of my life, to release all the negative emotions I'm still holding in my body and to feel the freedom and joy that I so clearly had that morning years ago when I left home. Today marks the prelude song for Cherise Shugar Brown's funeral that she was never afforded and since I never experienced a birthday party, I'll celebrate Shugar Brown's birth on that same day Cherise was silenced forever. Because who I was I could never be again….. you took that from me. However, I have to get on with my life and stop just existing in this world and start living. I need to love and feel love in return. I want affection and want to show affection. I want to make love to a man that loves me back, not because he sees me as a victim but because I'm a beautiful human being. And I need the pains in my stomach to finally go away and to do that I have to be allowed to get this hurt, these emotions, this shame, OUT of my body and mind. Being here today for me means I'm no longer going to be your victim but rather a survivor of a horrific crime. Today marks the beginning of that new normal for me.

If you are never allowed to walk the streets again as a free human being, I wouldn't care. Nor do I have an opinion on if you should be granted parole; that's the job of this Board to decide. But I will say that I am taking back my power from you and the other six of your co-defendants. Your faces have haunted me for years and so I'm divorcing myself from your ugliness and getting on with my life. I only hope that the impact of this crime against me is one day re-paid to you and you are forced to live this life of misery as I had."

6 JOURNAL ENTRY
March 3, 1998

It's been a long and strenuous day at work. With the new manager training program at the firm and starting college classes at night along with all the after school, after work, after Saturday nap and after Sunday activities, I'm so tired and worn out.

I still hadn't fully unpacked the boxes from my recent move to the little condo complex I moved myself and Stormy into. After that incident with the FBI busting down my mother's door, it was definitely time to get me and my baby out of that environment and move on.

Anyway, the last thing I want to do is stop by my mother's house just so she can tell me again why I should move Stormy and I back in with her or she should move with us to the little house I'm renting in Morristown. But I go to her house anyway; just to get it over with and to pick up Stormy after being over my Mom's all week to go to school.

"Ma! It's me" I yell as I come in and slam the back door behind me. Out of nowhere, here comes my chubby cheeks, pig-tails flying daughter, running in my direction and knocking the wind out of me. To my surprise, racing right behind her is a beautiful chocolate cocker spaniel puppy.

"Brownie!" Stormy says with open arms as her new friend jumps in her arms with tail wagging and tongue dripping with drool.

"Where did this little guy come from?" I ask.

"Her father and that girl Trina dropped that damn dog off here with Stormy when they brought her home from school today and I'm already tired from chasing behind him and that little face over there." My mother sounded really annoyed as she entered the room addressing me.

We both flop down on her leather couch and watch Stormy run off back up the stairs with her new puppy hot on her trail. So cute!

"So, what? Rick just drops off a dog with Stormy with no explanation? Like… what is this latest and greatest gift about and am I supposed to take this puppy home with me or is it supposed to live here with you?"

"Shugar. I don't know what it's supposed to mean. But lately, he or that little tramp of his, brings my grandbaby here every day with a new gift, toy, shoes, sneakers or jewelry and it don't make any damn sense. What he think? We don't take care of her or something or keep her looking nice enough? I told him today though that the damn dog was just too much and he need to stop all this foolishness. Spending all that money on an eight year old! What is trying to prove?"

"I wish I knew myself Mommy. It ain't so much that he buys her things all the time or that he wants to see her in beautiful clothes that bother me. The fact that he don't even bother to talk to me about her at all is what gets on my last nerve. I have asked Rick so many times to stop having that girl pick my baby up from school but he act like he don't hear me. So today I called the school and made sure no one is allowed to take her off the school campus that isn't on an approved list. Then I went ahead and filed for child support on him and I spoke to his parents about setting up scheduled visits for them and Stormy. Next week, I plan to file for full custody of her as well but I know Rick will fight me tooth and nail on that. But whatever."

At that moment, my mother looked at me a little sideways and twisted her face up at me. "Listen. I told you a long time ago to put papers on that boy but you had your nose so far up his ass you couldn't tell night from day. Now cause you done decided to move out, I guess you see it isn't as easy out there on your own trying to raise that baby without my help now is it?" She chuckled at her comment as if she was taking satisfaction in the thought that I was struggling and needed Rick's money or help to survive. Wow.

"Oh Mommy please! This don't have shit to do with me needing your help or Rick's money. What it's about is me finally growing up and taking care of my daughter like I'm supposed too. God! You act like I committed a crime cause I moved out. Damn! Get over it. I'm twenty-seven years old. It was time."

I am so upset with this constant innuendo that me moving out is some kind of curse on myself or something. Why can't this lady respect the fact that I'm growing up and moving on? You would think she would be happy for me but by the look of loathing on her face right now; happy is the last thing she feels for me.

"You are one ungrateful little girl. You know that

Shugar? I have done nothing but help you since you brought that little girl from the damn hospital. I changed my hours at work so you can work full-time and I can be home in time to help take care of my grandbaby. It was me who provided for the both of you when you couldn't do it. I provided the roof over your head and the food on the damn table every night. It was me who let you act a damn fool, running around here with boyfriend after boyfriend while Rick was away at school. All because you was having to deal with whatever affects you was supposed to be suffering from regarding that story about them boys touching on you a hundred years ago. And just because I worry about you and that baby, I told you stay here with me a little longer just so I know you raising her right and not filling her head with that mumbo-jumbo story about a damn gang rape. You wasn't fooling anybody with that damn story then and certainly not now. I know how you was sexing Rick and what have you Shugar! I know damn well that if seven men put they dicks inside you it was because you asked for it and Rick caught you doing it. So you said they took advantage of you but I know better and that's why he can't stand to be with you now and I can't blame him!"

I stood up from the couch with streams of hot tears running down my face and a broken heart. How could my own mother not believe that what happened to me was not my fault or that I didn't asked for it? After all these years she finally said what she felt too my face and I could barely keep the shaking of my body under control.

"Mommy? That's how you feel about me? You think I asked for those guys to rape me? To shred my insides to pieces? To humiliate and embarrass me the way they did in an open field? You really think that Rick caught me having sex with other men, outside mind you, and seven, eight years later he breaks up with me because of it? Really?"

"Shugar. You was starting to smell yourself back then and everybody saw it. Your little hips started spreading and your breasts were developing and everybody thought you was the most gorgeous thing and so did you. I saw how you was flirting with them boys then and I see how you got that Ibin's nose wide-open now. Like I said, you ain't fooling anybody but yourself."

My mother was sitting there with her arms folded, staring up at me and looking through me. I was not her child in this moment. And she wasn't my mother.

"I can't believe you're sitting in my face saying this shit to me right now. All because I moved out? And do you really think I would let something happen to my fuckn' daughter that I need to stay here so YOU can protect her? THOSE NIGGAHS RAPED ME! THEY FUCKIN' RAPED ME AND YOU NEVER DID OR SAID A DAMN THING ABOUT IT UNTIL NOW!!! BUT YOU BLAMING ME FOR IT; BASICALLY TELLING ME I DESERVED IT. WHAT KIND OF MOTHER ARE YOU?"

She was standing up now herself. Nose to nose with a lit cigarette pointed at my face.

"A damn good mother! I did everything I could for you! I took you back and forth to doctor's appointments and I bought you every book them people down at the clinic told me to get to help you so-call-cope. And I stopped sending you to that shrink cause she was making it seem like what I was doing wasn't enough. I knew what I was doing. Shit! When I was a little girl and my mother's 'friend' touched me, my mother didn't talk about it to me either and I was fine. So you was gonna be fine too. I did the best I could for you Shugar!"

"You didn't do shit for me! All you did do is treat me like I was invisible. Like what happened, didn't. Not one time did you ask me how I felt. I know why now. Cause you didn't even believe it happened. You never hugged me or consoled me. You never even asked to see my scars. You barely even talked to me since that day. I could never do that to my daughter. Never!"

WHAP! She slapped me across my face and pushed me to the corner of the living room as hard as she could. I was dazed at her physical reaction to this argument. But I pressed off the wall and pushed past her toward the door when I heard the crash of the flower vase hit the floor at my feet behind me. My mother threw it at my head and thankfully it missed.

I turned around and with fists balled, I was headed back towards her when I was then driven to the ground by my brother Jamal. He heard the arguing and yelling from outside and raced in the door and assumed I had thrown the vase at my mother.

Jamal had me pinned to the ground and was punching me in the back with his fists, yelling at me to don't ever disrespect his mother.

With every punch to my back, my head would slam against the hard wood floor. I finally managed to throw him off me and turn myself around to face him while still on the ground. All I could do is kick at him and scream for him to stop hitting me. Jamal was enraged and didn't care that he was fighting me like I was a man and not his sister.

After several more minutes of tussling with my brother, he and I were so tired from throwing punches and kicks that we stopped and I climbed off the floor with new lumps to my face and a busted lip. I looked over at my mother who had sat back down on the couch with the same lit cigarette staring in our direction. Jamal asked her what she wanted him to do with me. Can you believe it? I've somehow become enemy number one in my mother's house in a matter of minutes.

"You can kill that whore bitch for all I care." Was my mother's reply to Jamal as she sat back on the couch, crossed her legs and lit another cigarette. Right then, as far as I was knew, she was the devil and I wanted no parts of her. I needed to leave right now.

"Stormy! Stormy, time to go. Come on Baby. Where are you?" I'm running towards the stairs looking for my child so we can get the hell out of that house as fast as possible.

"I'm right here Mommy." Stormy's little voice came from behind the couch where my mother was sitting. My mother, brother and I all ran over towards her as she stood up with her own tears staining her small face and look of pure fright in her eyes. My baby was shaking like a leaf and couldn't move for the terror racking her body of what she had just witnessed.

My mother reached for her and Stormy grimaced; too afraid to let her take her hand or even embrace her. She didn't recognize her own grandmother immediately.

I walked over to her slowly myself, not knowing if she'd reject me too. I looked a mess. My hair was pulled apart and my clothes were all disheveled, twisted on my body. But she took my hand slowly and walked from behind the couch with Brownie following behind. I picked my daughter up in my arms and began walking out the door with the puppy obediently in tow.

Once I realized we were safe outside in my car, securely strapped in with the puppy in a seat belt as well, I locked my doors and let out a good hard cry right there. After about three minutes I started the car, put it in gear pulled off slowly from the street. Stormy reached over and placed her hand on my arm and said, "Mommy why is Grandma mad at you and make Jamal fight you?"

"It's big girl stuff Stormy. You're too little to understand right now but Grandma and Mommy love you and we didn't mean for you to see that." I'm sniffling; attempting to pull myself together so my daughter can be okay.

"I don't like it when Grandma look like that. She look like she had a mean mask on." Stormy says in a very low voice as if she is saying something so terrible.

How do you explain to a small child that witnessed her mother be a victim at the hands of a grandmother she loves dearly and an uncle she always looked up to as a hero? What am I supposed to say to her to make her feel better in this moment when I myself can't wrap my own understanding around what just happened?

"Don't worry Beloved. You won't ever have to see that mean mask on Grandma again."

The next day I receive several messages from my brother Ethan and sister Kyra asking me to call them back immediately. I'm sure they want to discuss what happened at Mommy's house but I had decided the night before after seeing my swollen face in the mirror that I wasn't going to talk to any one of them any time soon. After replaying over and over what my mother said to me in my head, I can't imagine how I can formulate the right words to get them to understand what really went down before the physical fight with me and Jamal.

The last of the six messages left today was from Jamal:

"Hello? Oh. It's the machine. Okay. Well anyway. It's Jamal again. Shugar, I was just calling to check on Stormy and to say I apologize for last night. I shouldn't have put my hands on you at all but when I was walking up to the house, all I heard was a bunch of yelling and screaming and then I heard a large crash and I thought somebody was attacking Mommy. Damn! I Feel real fucked up over this shit man. Ethan calling me threatening to fuck me up. Jamil called me collect and basically told me he gone get me killed if I didn't make this shit right and yo, his dude Ibin called me too and was talking real slick. Saying shit like if he was on the street he would make sure I ended up with a buck-fifty for what I did to you and shit. I'm sorry Shugar! I don't know what came over me. I don't know why I couldn't stop myself but when I looked over at Mommy….Word is bond she looked like pure evil and that's when I realized I fucked up. I fucked up bad. And after you left, she didn't say shit about it! She got up and started cooking cakes and pies and shit like it was nothing. I don't know yo, what's going on with her but I sincerely hope you accept my apology Shugar. For real. Let me make it up to you or something. Let me come out there and tell you face to face that I'm really sorry for doing that shit to you. Ah man; this is fucked up. Anyway…. I love you Sis and I'm sorry."

What the fuck ever! I have nothing to say to Jamal or my mother today, tomorrow or ever. As far as I'm concerned, they don't ever have to worry about seeing me or my daughter again. Fuck that. I cannot bring myself to forgive either one of them for yesterday. And my mother can simply forget it. The shit she said to me fucked my head up. That woman told me I asked to be gang raped! Humph. Unbelievable. My own mother. She thinks that I flirted my way into eight years of a silent turmoil. That idea is not easily exonerated and I'm not going back to pretending what happened to me didn't happen to suit her guilt.

After I call my manager and offer my version of the illness that is keeping me from coming back to work for the remainder of this week, I check on Stormy to ensure she is still asleep. My baby-girl is exhausted from the action she witnessed the day before. I think I'll keep her home from school with me and spend some quality time; just she and I. She deserves that after yesterday.

Now it's time to call Rick and make him aware of my plans going forward concerning our daughter.

"Hello Rick? This is Shugar.... Yeah I'm home and so is Stormy. What?..... No. I'm keeping her out of school for the rest of week. Even better, I'm going to transfer her to a school out here near home so you and your bitch don't have to worry about picking her up anymore and dropping her off to my mother's. ...... Why?..... Because that's what is best for her right now. I've asked you to stop having your chick pick my daughter up from school or changing her clothes every afternoon like Stormy is her personal dress-up doll but I see she never got that message. Furthermore, the schools are better out here where I am and she'll receive a better education. ..... Really? I can't do that without talking to you?... HA! I'm talking to you now and since we are talking, I might as well tell you that I'm filing for child support and requesting full custody of Stormy. And because I'm already on a roll, you should know that under no circumstances going forward is my daughter to ever be alone in a car, in your house, your parent's house or any other place or space alone with Trina. Do you understand that?.... Oh you don't? Well, let me help you to understand it better.

I'm over you. I'm over the bullshit you put me through these last couple of years and I'm done chasing you and I'm done playing games with you. You will see your daughter on a regular basis and you will spend quality time with her whenever I need you too or she asks too. You will help me raise our daughter in a manner that will produce a healthy and happy adult. When I call you, it will be only to discuss the rearing of our daughter and nothing else. Furthermore, you will answer each of my calls or run the risk of dealing with me in court or in person and you are not going to like that one bit. There. Did that help you better grasp what this is about?.... Silence. That's what I thought. I will see you in two weeks when I drop our daughter off to you at your parent's home. Goodbye." Click.

7 JOURNAL ENTRY
April 1, 1998

Spring is definitely in the air as my new girlfriend and I observe leaving the gym we recently joined. It's about seventy-two degrees out and having just finished a serious cardio workout in the gym, it feels good to experience such a warm breeze so early in the season.

The YMCA had a membership deal in my township and since I met my neighbor Kisha, we decided to register together and workout as a team to motivate one another. Her son and my daughter are the same age and attend the same school together so it has been great having someone available to pick Stormy up from after care and take care of her until I arrive home every evening. This way, Stormy and Jason have play time together daily and she is right next door from my own home.

It's been about a month since I've seen or spoken to my mother or brother Jamal. I've only taken one or two calls from my sister Kyra or and my uncle James has called several times over the weeks all in an attempt to get me my mom and I to reconcile. But I'm not interested in the least.

I have my moments when I feel awful for Stormy who

expresses daily how much she misses her grandmother but I make it my business to ensure that Rick as least shares his weekends with my mother whenever he needs to run an errand or just wants a break himself. It's not nearly as much as she is used to seeing my mother but it will have to do.

My mother hasn't bothered to call once herself to apologize or to see how I was dealing with all of this which leads me to believe it doesn't faze her at all. She's always had a tough exterior when it came to admitting her own feelings about someone or something.

Since my father moved away from us when I was three years old, she's been a cold and distant person. I personally believe she's lonely but because she had small children at home when he left, she never had any intentions of bringing another man, who wasn't our father, into the mix and I totally understand that.

My family is the kind that keeps a lot of very old secrets you know? For instance, I don't even know if my parents were ever married at some point in their relationship. No one talks about it and if you ask her she'll just say it's none of our business what she did or who she did it with. My mother had five children of her own, all by my father but he had eight additional children by three other women. Those children, our step brothers and sisters are either the same age as many of my mother's children or a year or two younger than some of us. This means that my dad had his share of women all up and in between his courtship with Sheila Roberts; my mother.

Yet, she never spoke ill of my father. In fact, she never spoke of him at all. Ever. When he came around or called to tell us happy birthday or during holiday time, my mother wouldn't even bother to talk to him to ask for money or assistance of any kind. She went out of her way, seems like, to avoid having interaction with him at all.

Since I can remember, she has worked at the big insurance company downtown as a Benefits Specialist Manager. At the age of forty-three she went back to school and earned her bachelor's degree in business management and she was six months shy of earning her master's degree when I was brutally attacked.

Twelve weeks into my healing, I discovered I was pregnant with Stormy and my mother dropped out of graduate school to dedicate herself to ensuring I met my psych visits and now pre-natal appointments. I had such a hard pregnancy because my body wasn't near capable of sustaining an unborn child without total and complete bed rest. That required my mother to be at my beckon call around the clock to look after me and take special care of me.

It didn't appear she mind putting in that effort to help her daughter. My mother wasn't a coddler or the hugging and kissing type. She just wasn't that woman but she did do everything in her power to make sure I was comfortable at all times and taking my medications as instructed. She even took a leave of absence from work the last three months of my pregnancy and then six additional weeks after Stormy was born to stay by my side.

When Stormy arrived, it was then I saw the softest side of my mom. Her eyes lit up whenever my daughter cooed or reached in her direction. You can tell that Stormy being born was the high light of her life during that time. She doted on her constantly and would even sit up with her at night when she was colic and wouldn't sleep. Her only granddaughter was her pride and joy and she gave my mother purpose again.

There were moments I would sit and stare at my mother interact with my own daughter and would become aggressively jealous of their relationship. It was so hard to accept that my mother could be so loving and show so much affection to Stormy, who wasn't her daughter, than she could to me. But then I would always find myself being grateful that my daughter knew such unconditional love. I certainly was not feeling that way.

It was around 6:05 pm when I answered an anonymous call on my house phone. Someone named Trish was calling me on a three way with a collect call from my brother Jamil.

"Hey Shugar. How are you and Stormy doing?" Jamil was so excited to speak to me. Instantly, I began to tear up from just the sound of his voice. Finally I was talking to someone I didn't declare my enemy.

"Hey Jamil! I'm fine. Stormy is fine too. What is going on with you? Did you go to court yet?" I'm so fervent to get answers to so many questions.

"Yeah Shugg. We went to court last week. Mommy didn't tell you? I got three years and Ibin got a year. He should be out this summer though. He don't have priors so he good. But that's not what I called you for; I don't want to talk about me and my situation. What's going on with you and Mommy? I heard what happened and that's fucked up. You alright?" I gotta love my brother. In spite of what he is going through, he has room enough in his heart to be more concerned with what is going on with me.

"It is what it is Jamil. I'm good. I'll get over it

eventually. But the messed up part is that she hasn't called me one time to see how I was doing or to talk to Stormy. I know she sees Stormy whenever Rick drops her off to the house but she gotta know that she cries for her just about every night. Shit. I cry for her too but I know she won't call me." I can't help but break down thinking about this.

"Listen. Mommy got some issues with her Shugar and it's real fucked up all the she shit she said and what she made Jamal do but she love you though. I mean, Daddy put her through some fucked up shit too and the fact that she had to raise her own brothers and sisters since she was like what, 15 years old, I don't think she ever knew how to just be. You know what I'm saying? She, she, just had it rough and she couldn't be soft so she always had to be hard. But I know she loves us though or she couldn't have been a good mother. And you gotta admit, Sheila did right by us Shugar. We ain't ever been hungry or without anything and she did that shit on her own with no help from her sperm donor. I ain't saying what happened ain't fucked up; it is. But Yall gotta fix this shit."

"Jamil. I understand what you are saying but Mommy....she hurt me. She hurt me deep and I know Jamal is feeling bad for the part he played but I can't figure out how to get past this. For years, I lived my life and pretended like what happened didn't happen all for the sake of everybody else. No one would talk about it so I didn't talk about it. People didn't want to hear all the pain those niggahs put me through or the hurt I had to endure afterwards or how dogged out I felt by Rick and how he treated me emotionally all the years following. And the one person I needed to hear me wouldn't. Mommy couldn't, no she wouldn't be there for me because deep down inside she felt like I deserved it. How do I get over that Jamil? How?"

"I don't know Shugar but try… for me. Anyway, somebody wants to say hi to you. Hold on." I can hear the phone rustling between hands.

"Hello?" It's Ibin.

"Hello. This is Shugar. Who is this?"

"It's Ibin. How are you?"

"I'm fine Ibin. How are you?

"I'm good but I don't have a lot of time so I'm just gone get right too it. (He takes a deep breath) Shugar I heard what happened between you and your Mom's and your brother and I think it's real fucked up, you feeling like you out there on your own having to deal with shit like that without no real support. But I wanted to tell you that what I know about you is that you strong and you can get through anything you put your mind too. I got a feeling you're going be aight.

That's not all I wanted to say though. (Pause) Shugar, I wanted to tell you that the few months I been in here, the only thing that keeps me sane in this cage is remembering that kiss. Hunh. All these years, since I first saw you, I been wanting you in my life and I finally got to kiss you and I'd swear on a stack of bibles that it was the best feeling in the world. (He chuckles) Shit. I was the only one in that truck that night we got hemmed up, grinning like a fucking idiot; still tasting your lips on my mouth. Them niggahs thought I was crazy. (His voice trails off before speaking again) Hold on a sec. I'm just looking around making sure your brother walked away before I say this….. when I told you I love you Shugar, I meant it. I'm falling in love with you. And before you say anything about that, I want you to know that I know you don't feel the same way and that's okay. But I know it's love. It's love you because I'm feeling like a feign in here. I just want to see you. I want to protect you. I want to kiss you again. And I know how you feel out there. Like your back is to the wall and your friends are few; you don't trust anybody.

But no matter what you say after this, I want you know that you got me. If nothing else, I'ma have your back. And when I get outta here, I'ma prove it too you cause I know you need that. (Pause) That's it."

There is a long silence on the phone except for the music in the background from Trish's house where she probably just set the phone down somewhere while we use her three-way to speak to one another.

Think of something to say Shugar. Think of something…fuck it, I'ma say it.

"Ummm. Ok. Well, I'm not gonna pretend it's not a good thing to hear that someone loves me Ibin. I appreciate you telling me that but really, we only shared a kiss and maybe some flirting here and there. And I'm not gonna lie; it was a good kiss. But Ibin, you don't want anybody as messed up as I am. You are young and when you come home, you have a chance to make things right and get your life in order. But we can definitely be friends however, we should not have kissed. I don't know why I kissed you back yet I don't regret it. I'm thinking we should forget about it and you need to concentrate on getting out of there. So if you need anything, you can call me collect directly. Ok?"

Ibin starts to laugh quietly into the receiver. "Shugar, I didn't expect you to say anything other than what you just said. And like I said, that's okay. I understand and I'm glad you said we can at least be friends when I come home. I'm good with that. You just be good out there and take good care of that little girl.."

"I will. Bye."

I sit on my couch trying to decipher how I feel about what Ibin just said to me. He loves me? But why? We haven't had sex or anything. The most we've done is kiss in my mother's house and that was months ago. How could he say that he loves me?

I have to admit that over the past couple of months before they were locked up, I have felt a little attraction for him from time to time. Not like a love different but a different different. I mean, he is the only person who let me tell him all about the gang rape from beginning to end and he didn't stop me once nor did he cringe at all the disgusting details. Ibin listened to me so intently and with great dedication to hear it to the end that I felt comfortable enough to be vulnerable around him. I had never been that kind of content with another human being in my life. He made it so easy for me to be me. But. He is so not for me. Ibin is young and stupid; out there selling drugs and wasting his life. I can't get involved in anything like that. I am though, going to be his friend.

8 JOURNAL ENTRY
June 21, 1998

I honestly cannot take another morning of little Miss Stormy's constant whining for her Nanna; my mother. I could be brushing her hair, taking off her shoes or just watching a children's program with her and somehow she goes into this annoying insistent cry about wanting to see her. Ugghhh!

I realize it's not her fault that my mother and I are having a hard time getting along right now. Besides, Stormy has broken me down with that sweet, sweet face of hers. How can I deny her? But to have her see my mother would mean I have to see my mother as well. To do that, I will have to muster every ounce of pride and humbleness I have to even fix my brain to have any kind of conversation with that woman. For my daughter, I will try. Of course I will.

Before I can park my car in front of my mom's house, Stormy is already unbuckling the seat belt from her car seat and unlocking the back door to get out. Thank goodness, the child-safety lock is on or she would have fell out onto the sidewalk. I haven't seen my baby so excited in quite some time and I have to admit it's good to see her smile again.

As I close the driver's side door and open the back door to help Stormy out of the car, I don't even notice Ibin's mother, Mona approach my car.

"Excuse me. Shugar?" I turn to face her.

"Hi. I don't know if you remember me but Ibin is my son and he runs for your brother Jamil."

"Hi Ms. Mona. Yeah, I remember who you are. How is Ibin doing?" I'm assuming she has approached me to ask for money for drugs.

Stormy is pulling my hand and very anxious to get to her grandmother's home though, but I ignore her constant pull on my arm. I am not as anxious as Stormy to see Sheila so it can wait until I'm done stalling talking to Ibin's mother.

"He is doing fine; ready to come home of course. He ain't never did time before so he ain't use to jailing. In fact, Ibin ain't ever been in trouble before now. His father raised that boy to be a Man and be a stand up person. But after them dudes killed him, it's like me and Ibin was just lost. Bull, that's my husband's name, Bull took care of everything. I didn't have to do nothing and Ibin didn't want for anything. Hell. Bull was our world…. Then they shot my man right between his eyes and now he gone. (She wipes her eyes as if she is wiping away a tear but there is no tear to speak of) And I got on this shit and Ibin had to take care of me at 15 years old."

Ms. Mona starts to stare off a little into her own thoughts and I realize this isn't a conversation my daughter needs to be privy too. I decide to get to the point and end this dialogue with her so I can get on to the business of dealing with my own mother.

"Ms. Mona, I got five dollars you are welcomed too if that will help but I gotta get my baby in the house so she can pee." I throw in my best chuckle to seal the deal.

She looks up at me with a bit of surprise in her face and puts her hands on her hips.

"I don't want your money Shugar. Want I wanted to tell you is that my son likes you. Rather, he loves you and I've seen how you prance around here all high and mighty about yourself and that's cool. Cause if you don't think you the shit, no one else will either. However, my son is the only good thing in this world I have left and the last thing I want to see is him hurt. Now. When he comes home in a couple of weeks, I'ma need you to stay far away from Ibin so he don't put all his concentration into trying to impress you just to keep your attention. You don't want him. Fine. But he is a good and loyal man just like his Daddy and he deserves to be with someone who loves him the same way. Don't hurt my son. I hope I made myself clear because I don't repeat myself." But then she pauses and looks me up and down as if she just remembered something else she wanted to say.

"One more thing. My son told me about what happened to you when you was younger and I feel sorry for you. Nobody should have to ever suffer at another person's hands that way. But just like I don't know your struggles, you don't know mine. So before you decide you know my story because it's known I have a habit, you should know this is not who I want to be. I cry every time I take a pull from a pipe because I know I'm not the same mother that birthed that beautiful man that has his nose open for the likes of you. Humph. We all do things we ashamed of and regret. And I will die regretting some of the mistakes I made. Just like the men, or at least one of the men that raped you, died regretting the mistake he made in hurting you. Forgive the rest of them anyway. "

I'm a bit shocked and annoyed that this woman would find the nerve to speak to me this way. I stare at her for a few minutes but then I reply halfhearted.

"I hear you Ms. Mona. I will stay away from your son. And I will consider forgiving the men that hurt me but that's a tall order."

With that, she yells for her scruffy dirty little dog and walks off.

As I knock on my mother's door, my heart is pounding and I feel like I want to throw up. What is taking her so long to get to the damn door?

I hear someone approaching finally and the door is unlocked and slowly opens. It's my brother Jamal and he looks just as nervous as I to see me on the other side of the door. But it doesn't surprise me that my mother would have someone else answer knowing I was on my way. That's just how she is; always controlling the situation to benefit her. Never giving up ground. Clever.

"Uncle Jamal!" Stormy screams as she jumps up into his arms. She immediately buries her face in his shoulders and begins to cry. Awww. She missed her uncle. Jamal is just as happy to see his niece. "Look at Uncle's little princess! How are you Stormy? How have you been?" Jamal swings her around and plants kiss after kiss on her face and tickles her tummy to help loosen her grip around his neck. Stormy giggles with such glee. It's beautiful to watch her be so happy because she is finally back at Nanna's house.

"Is that my Stormy Waters I see over there?" my mother

proclaims as she walks into the living room where I am still in the doorway. Too frightened to move from this spot in front of the closed door.

"Nanna!" Stormy shouts for her grandmother and jumps out of Jamal's arm and runs towards my mother. But she stops short at my mother's feet.

"Nanna? You still mad at me from before?" Stormy looks up and asks that question with such sincerity in her eyes.

"No Stormy! Nanna was never mad with or upset with her Stormy. Are you kidding me? How can a Nanna be mad at a Stormy?"

A huge smile breaks across my baby girl's face and all is right in her world again. But hello... what about me? I mean, I'm standing right here and no one has acknowledged me at all.

Suddenly, my sister Kyra comes jumping down the stairs, past my mother and pulls me into a bear hug with her and I can let out a much needed exhale.

I hug Kyra back and before I can command them to stop, the tears begin to roll down my face. It feels so good to be this close to anyone from my family again. I love Kyra. And without a doubt Kyra loves me in return.

As I make every attempt of pulling myself together, Jamal takes me by the hand and leads myself and Kyra into the dining room while my mother and Stormy remain in the living room to catch up.

"Shugar. I'm sorry. I'm sorry for attacking you. I'm sorry for not being man enough to stop and take inventory of what was really happening that night and I'm sorry I wasn't a better brother. Can you forgive me?" Jamal has a look of earnestness on his face I cannot deny and I melt. The truth is, I miss my brother's presence in mine and my daughter's life and I would do almost anything to have him be back a part of our lives; except forgive him.

"I accept your apology Jamal and I appreciate hearing directly from you." My sister grabs my hand across the table as if to stop me from finishing my thought. But I continue.

"However, what you did to me that day hurt me to my heart. Not because you harmed me physically, but because you treated me like the enemy. Me Jamal! Without even knowing what was going on you pounced all over me and beat me to a pulp. I can't forget that. I can't forget that I'm your sister and like those guys who raped me, you too beat a piece of my soul to oblivion, never to return. I'm sorry."

Kyra throws her hands up to her mouth in shock and shakes her head back and forth as she searches both mine and Jamal's face for reaction to what was just said.

"I understand Shugar and I can accept that." Was all Jamal retorted. He looked crushed and I felt the way he looked.

"Okay then. I'm going to grab Stormy and we are going to be on our way home now." I suddenly felt a huge urge to leave my mother's home after only a few minutes.

The feeling of anxiety was beginning to overwhelm me and I had no explanation for it except I felt totally uncomfortable and needed to leave right away.

"Shugar?" Kyra stood up with me and reached out to me for an embrace. But I couldn't do it.

"Don't touch me Kyra!" I barked.

"I have to go. I have to go right now. Where is my daughter?" The anxiousness had reached my throat and I was ready to throw up where I stood.

Kyra backed away with tears in her eyes and in that moment and for the first time ever, I didn't care about her feelings. I just needed to leave.

I walked as fast as I could towards the front of the house where my mother and Stormy were sitting on the couch playing Miss Mary Mack. I grabbed my daughter by her hand and pulled her off the couch and towards the door.

"What is going on Shugar?" My mother's face was stunned at this sudden display of anger.

"Didn't Jamal apologize to you? Why are you snatching the baby up like that? You just got here."

"Yes! Jamal did apologize and you didn't so much as even look my way. I don't know. I don't feel comfortable here anymore. We have to go. I'm sorry." I grab the door knob ad begin to turn as my mother grabs my free arm.

"Shugar..... I'm... " she pauses and stares into my face and abruptly lets my arm go. "Never mind."

Stormy and I step off the porch and head towards the door. I can't explain in this moment what I'm feeling like except its pure panic. I'm not sure what I panicking about or why I couldn't accept Jamal's apology and move on.

As I buckle Stormy in her car seat and throw myself into the driver's seat, I begin to feel my racing heart slow down to a more normal rhythm and I realize I was hyper-ventilating. What the hell happened? Why did I react that way?

9 JOURNAL ENTRY
August 15, 1998

Waking up to a constant ringing phone this early in the morning with a nauseating migraine is not my idea of a great start to a Saturday morning. Whomever this is has been calling me back to back since 6:30 this morning and its only 9:30 now. Ridiculous!

But I can't take it anymore. Whoever the caller, won't leave a message on the answering machine and my caller ID keeps reading 'Caller Unknown' in the display.

Obviously, my "friend", Nasir can't take the constant ringing either as he looks over to my bloodshot eyes while handing me the receiver.

"HELLO!" I answer the phone with absolute venom so as to make it clear to whoever is on the other end that I am not in a good mood and this call had better be worth the wrath they are about to receive for calling me this damn early on what is supposed to be a day for me to sleep in.

"Good morning. I'd like to speak with a Miss Shugar Brown please. This is Warden Parker of the Federal BOP located in Pittsburgh." Said this forceful woman's voice. I knew she was calling me from the Federal Bureau of Prisons where my brother was staying but what this could be about, I was wondering.

"Yes. This is Miss Brown. How can I help you Warden Parker? Is my brother Jamil okay?"

"Mam, I calling you today because I have a Mr. Ibin Trina in my office to speak with you regarding an urgent matter. Will you accept the call Miss Brown?"

"Yes of course." Was my immediate reply. In the next instance, Ibin was on the line.

"Ibin are you okay? Did something happen to Jamil?" I was firing off rapid questions to Ibin as I sat up completely in my bed and clutched my hands to my chest while my visiting friend, Nasir was now sitting up as well. He was trying to make some since of this one way conversation he was hearing.

"Calm down Shugar. Jamil is okay and so am I… kinda. I'm calling you from the Warden's office because I was called down here to find out that my mother died yesterday."

I was stunned by the news Ibin was delivering to me with such calmness in his voice.

"I'm sorry Ibin. Wow. What happened?" was all I could think of to say in that moment. I instantly felt so terrible for him. Ibin and his mom appeared to be very close for mother and son.

"I really don't have a lot of time to explain over the phone right now but after I was told about my mom, they let me make a personal call to my grandmother and to you. My Grandma told me they going to bury my Mom next week because arrangements have to be made for me to see her by the prison and that's why I'm calling you."

"Okay Ibin. What do you need me to do?"

"Shugar, they said I can come to the funeral home to view my mother one last time but I have to be brought there before the actual funeral starts and before everyone else will be there. Not only that though, I will have a prison guard with me the whole time but I can invite one other person to sit with me the one hour I get to be with her and I'm hoping you can be that one person."

Ibin sounds so very sure of what he was asking me and he didn't sound emotional. I wonder if he is being this way for my sake or because he is where he is.

"Are you sure you want me to be there Ibin? Don't you want to have your grandmother there or maybe one of your aunts or cousins or somebody?"

"I'm sure I want you to be there Shugar. And if it can't be you then I will do this alone. Can you come?"

I take a deep breath and say, "Yes."

"Okay. Well Warden Parks or somebody from this office will call you back with all the details and I guess I'll see you at the funeral home. Thank you Shugar." With that the line went dead and I sat on my bed still stunned at the news that Ibin's mother is dead. Wow.

Nasir looked up at me again with inquisitive eyes; asking what happened without uttering a word. I lean into his bare chest and begin to explain what I knew and who Ibin was in relation to my brother. When I was done explaining, Nasir shrugged his shoulders and began to pat me on the back as I attempted to process the entire conversation and then attempt sleep one more time.

This time, I'm in a dark hallway in some kind of abandoned building and I'm standing in about an inch of water. There is a very dim light coming from a cracked door down the corridor and I'm walking towards it. As I approach the open entry to this empty apartment, I hear men talking in a low whisper in a room towards the back of this space. I slide my body into the apartment without making any noise and I creep in the direction of the hushed conversation.

I make out one voice and it's very familiar but I can't figure out who it is and then there is three more voices and two I don't recognize at all. But one voice I identify as Rick's.;

"...naw Man! You have to make it look like it was a coincidence. Damn! You are going to fuck the whole thing up being greedy!" Rick was telling the huddle of men.

They were all standing around in a small tight circle pointing and staring at the other. I could only see Rick from this angle and he looks upset by the conversation. I can see that his right eye is swollen shut and his lip is busted while he wipes his bloody nose with the back of his hand.

I take another step to better position my left foot in the water because I feel like I'm standing on a rock. I look down and see blood pouring down my legs and I have no pants or underwear on. And upon further inspection of my body, I realize I'm totally naked with cuts and bruises up and down my arms and legs but I don't feel pain at all.

All of a sudden an older woman comes out of nowhere and heads straight towards me. Only, she is holding a dirty yellow blanket out to me.

"Here Shugar. Stop tempting them boys and put this blanket around your naked body 'fore they come and get some more of you! Didn't your mother teach you better than that?"

Just then, Rick and the others hear her talking to me and they look up and heads my way in the open doorway. I'm terrified as I grasp at the idea that I'm in a lot of trouble yet I can't move! I stand there in one spot frozen stiff as I stare back at all these faces. Tears begin to fill my eyes and my bottom lip starts to quiver.

Rick stops in front of me and says, "Shugar. This is fucked up, I know. I couldn't stop them though Shugar. You believe me right? I couldn't stop them. You should have just did what I asked and this wouldn't have happened." His eyes are pitch black and full of water.

He stretches out his hand and offers me my torn and bloodied underwear. But I turn my head in the direction of someone yelling in the hallway.

"FIRE! FIRE! FIIIRREE!"

Nasir is shaking me violently out of my nightmare and I'm throwing weak punches to get him off me. When I'm fully awaken, I'm embarrassed that Nasir has a look of 'what the fuck?' in his own eyes while he tries to stop my failing arms.

I give up the fight and I collapse back on his chest and cry as hard as I could until my voice goes hoarse.

After about an hour, Nasir climbs out of the bed and retrieves a wet wash cloth from my bathroom and wipes my puffy face. I know I have to tell him what the nightmare was about and why I even have nightmares to begin with but I'm not looking forward to it.

Finally, I meet someone I like and I'm praying he likes me just as much. Nevertheless, telling him my story may turn him off.

After I'm finally composed, I commence talking and he

listens as intently as he could until it got too graphic. Nasir put his hand on my mouth to stop me from telling him anymore about that night. He says he gets the picture and I don't have to say anymore because he doesn't want to make me relive it. But really, he can't handle hearing about seven men viciously attacking me.

Yet, he swaddles me in his arms and comforts me for hours afterwards right there in my bedroom. Just the two of us. No TV, no phone calls, no Stormy.

Nasir kisses my lips softly. He tells me I'm a strong black woman for having dealt with what I did and surviving it. He called me a survivor.

I think I'm falling in love!

10 JOURNAL ENTRY
August 19, 1998

Walking into the funeral home was totally creepy and unnerving for me but I found my way to the smallest chapel in the building and saw Ibin sitting there with his shoulders hunched low and his chin in his chest. I walked slowly towards him although I don't think he had noticed that I had arrived.

After showing two pieces of identification and allowing my purse to be rummaged through before entering this small space where Miss Mona was nicely laid to rest, it was all I could do to keep from wrapping my arms around Ibin's shoulders and consoling him. But I didn't. I quietly sat directly behind him until he finally lifted his head and turned in his seat to acknowledge me. Ibin, with red and swollen eyes, gave me a nod and turned back to face his mother.

I gently placed a hand on his shoulder and sympathetically patted him as a gesture of condolence. Ibin embraced my fingers in his hand, without turning to face me again and kissed my palm.

The correction officer who accompanied Ibin finally approached me and asked if I was Cherise Brown; I admitted that was my government name and attempted to smile him away. Instead, he introduced himself as Officer Booth and offered me a look of interest. Without interrupting Ibin's time of mourning, I shot him a look of 'are you serious?' and he got the message. Officer Booth announced to Ibin he had thirty minutes left before we both had to leave.

Another ten minutes had lapsed with the three of us in this room sitting in silence except for the weird funeral home music that is played throughout.

I decided I should say something at this point so I lean from behind into Ibin's ear and ask if he's okay. He waves for me to come and sit next to him and I oblige.

"Ibin…is there anything I can do?" It seemed like the appropriate thing to as. He turns his handsome face towards mine and slowly shakes his head no.

I felt useless. This man was hurting for his mother and I didn't know what to say or how I can be of any comfort. I couldn't bring myself to look at his her lying in the coffin. This is a situation I cannot even imagine happening to me and here I am not knowing what to do next.

I slipped my hand in between his huge paws that were laced together between his knees. Ibin allowed my fingers to intertwine with his and he gave them a little squeeze. In that instant, I felt like I was helping ease his pain some.

"Shugar. Why did you come here today?" Ibin's voice startled me because I wasn't expecting him to speak at all.

In a very meek voice I answered, "Because you asked me too Ibin." But I was confused by the question.

"I know I asked you to come but why did you agree to do it?"

"The truth?" Was my reply.

"Yeah, the truth." Our hands are clutched tight together and Ibin is studying our fingers.

"Because I felt like you needed me here. I'm not sure why you wanted me to be here but because you asked too, I came." That was my truth.

I honestly felt drawn to this man for some reason and when he invited me to be with him when he'd see his mother for the last time, I felt obligated to grant him that.

"You are a beautiful woman Shugar. I don't mean just physically but your being is beautiful and I love you for doing this."

I can tell Ibin had more to say so I sat quietly with my hand still in his and waited patiently.

"My mother was my everything. You understand? That woman had my back 100% and I know she loved me unconditionally. She is all I had in this world and I'm going to miss her like crazy. But after my father died, she had made up hcr mind to leave this earth too and I'm not mad at her Shugar.

I hated seeing her like that... a crackhead. It killed me slowly everyday she had to be out there living like that. My job was to protect her but then I got locked up and look what happened. It's fucked up. I wish she had gotten to see us be together. That way, she would have died knowing I'ma be okay." Ibin began to shake his head from side to side again slowly; thinking and remembering.

"But Ibin, Sweetheart…. We are not together." I scrunched my eyebrows, trying to make sense of what he is saying.

"I don't mean today but one day. One day, you goin' to be my wife and have my kids and I needed her to know that was gonna happen so she can be alright up in heaven."

Deciding to appease him in his time of grief was the best thing I can do. "She is always going to be with you so if we are meant to be then she knows that and will be around to witness it."

"I love you Shugar." He was looking me straight in my eyes.

Without knowing I'd ask the question, it came stumbling out, "You have been saying that for months and the most we've done is shared a kiss. How can you love me? Why do you keep saying that?"

I didn't mean to come off as annoyed but I was intrigued by his consistency.

"I love you beyond a reason why Shugar. I just do."

He took both my hands in his and we both turned towards the coffin again as it was being closed by the funeral directors.

Correction Officer Booth stood in front of both Ibin and I and explained we had a few minutes to say goodbye and that I had to leave the chapel first before Ibin was put back in leg irons and handcuffs to be exported back to the prison camp.

As we stood face to face for the first time since we kissed at my mother's house, Ibin had a look of relief on his face. I asked if he was okay.

"I'm good Shugar. You came."

I smiled at him and placed my hand on the side of his face and he turned his head to kiss the palm of my hand again.

"Take care of yourself in there Ibin and let me know if there is anything I can do. Okay?"

"Can I write you until I come home? I only got a couple more months."

"Sure Ibin. You can write me." It's the least I can do.

With that, he kissed me on my forehead and told me to leave now.

When I reached my car outside, I regretted not telling him I had met someone I was totally falling for and him writing me may not be appropriate for my new relationship. But as I entered the apartment and saw Nasir comfortably awaiting my arrival on my living room couch and felt the remnants of Ibin's fingers laced in mine, I changed my mind about regretting it. I'm relieved I didn't tell him.

11 JOURNAL ENTRY
October 18, 1998

"What kind of bullshit are you on Shugar, moving some niggah in with my fucking daughter hunh? If you thought for one fucking minute I was gonna let that shit slide, you were sadly mistaken!" Rick was standing in my doorway furious and yelling at the top of his lungs.

"First of all Rick, you need to calm the fuck down before you get both of our asses locked up for disorderly conduct or some shit like that. These white people around here do not take kindly to people who look like us disturbing their peace. Secondly, why don't you try stepping inside and talking to me like the adult I am." This fool must have me confused me with someone else, thinking he's gonna talk to me any old kind of way.

Rick takes my advice and steps all the way into mine and Nasir's apartment and I close the door behind him hoping to discuss whatever his issues are calmly and without incident. However, that will be a stretch for Rick because these days, since finding out I was in a serious relationship with someone else, he's been acting very irrational and irritated all the time.

"Okay. Now what seems to be your problem Rick?" I ask as he crudely takes a seat on the leather Italian sofa he seems to be admiring.

"OUR daughter told me and my girl this morning that you moved your boyfriend, of what, six months in with you and her but you didn't bother to tell me about it. I have a problem with that. I don't want no other niggah living with my daughter at her age Shugar."

I thought his comments were funny at best and I intend to call him on it. But before I do, I had to admit to myself that Rick is looking mighty fine lately. He's put on a little weight and clearly started working out. His body appeared to be tight but not overly muscular. Not to mention, he had allowed his goatee to grow in completely and had it trimmed to perfection.

Since our last big argument, I had kept a solid distance from him and his girlfriend on purpose. I drop Stormy off to him curbside at his or his parent's home and when I pick her up they do the same in return. The arrangement has been working out great thus far and so I hadn't noticed the recent change in Rick's physique as of late. Not bad if I must say so myself. But he appeared to be checking me out too from the looks he was giving me; he sizing me up.

"So yes. I have been dating Nasir for a little minute now and yes, he has moved in with Stormy and I. But I do not feel like you were owed a vote in that matter. From what I know from OUR daughter, your little chica has been living with you for well over a year now and I haven't asked you about it once. OUR daughter has never come home and complained about your girl mistreating or talking sideways to her and so as far as I'm concerned, it was none of my business as I have no have apprehensions. What you do in your home is your business as long as OUR daughter is taken care of in a manner befitting a child her age considering you are the parent. Therefore, the same respect should be given to me in my home. Has Stormy complained about Nasir to you at all when she discussed with you him moving in?"

"No. She wasn't complaining but I don't think that shit is cool. She is a young female and ain't no niggah gonna be living with my child at her age that is not her father. Period." Rick was not trying to hear what I was saying.

"There is no period Rick." At this point I'm growing angrier by the minute.

"I do not need to check in with you before having my boyfriend move in with me. Stormy may be your daughter but she is my full-time responsibility and I wouldn't dare move any person, man or woman, in with me unless I knew for sure my child was safe. Nasir has proven to me that he can be trusted to be around OUR daughter and because we are in a serious committed relationship we thought it was a good idea that we shared a home with yours and my daughter. You don't need to be okay with that at all but you will need to respect it and keep your comments about it too Stormy to a bare minimum." There! How about that for telling this asshole off? How dare he come into my home and tell me who I can and can't have living with me. He must've lost his damn mind.

"Oh. So that little street niggah, Ibin can tell you I'm not allowed to come around your old neighborhood to see you and my daughter but I can't tell you who I don't want around my daughter? Yeah I heard about that corny shit back then. But that's how it works Shugar? A dude gotta be fucking you to tell you what is right and what is wrong in your world?"

No he didn't! This fool is not sitting up here with his feet on my floor calling me a sideline whore on the sneak.

Luckily for Rick, Nasir is unlocking the front door and interrupting our argument. It makes me a bit nervous initially to have my new boyfriend meet my ex-boyfriend and the father of my daughter in an unexpected happenstance but Nasir is a mature man and prayerfully, he won't allow this incident to rattle him.

"Hey Baby." Nasir enters the apartment and plants a sensuous kiss on my lips as he greets me before turning to extend a hand to Rick for a handshake. He introduces himself.

"Hello. I'm Nasir Carlisle, Shugar's boyfriend, but please feel free to call me Nas."

Rick shook his hand and seemed to be admiring Nasir now as he stood eye to eye with him in this space.

Nasir continued, "I was approaching the door and couldn't help but overhear your heated discussion with my lady over the living arrangements here. I'd like to interject if you'd be so inclined to hear me out... Rick is it?"

Hmm, mmm, mmm. Is all my mind could come up with as I watched my very handsome man swoop in and act all calm and manly in a very nicely tailored Brooks Brother's navy blue suit as well as those buffed to perfection Cole Haan shoes. Damn! My baby looked good and smelled even better. I'm gonna enjoy Rick's reaction to Nasir's approach.

I cross my arms and turn towards my 'baby-daddy' just in time to see the veins pop out of his forehead.

"Yes. My name is Rick. Nice to meet you Nasir Carlisle. And I was just explaining to my ex-girlfriend that I was not comfortable with you moving in with her and my daughter so soon after meeting one another. I am more uncomfortable with the fact that she hadn't talked to me about the living arrangements over here before you all made it happen. So what's up?" Rick was definitely attempting to hold his own on this one.

"What's up is that I met Shugar a few months back and your daughter and I were introduced to one another once we decided we were dating exclusively. I will admit though that things moved a bit fast for all of us but we both sat Stormy down, once it was decided we'd wanted to live together, and talked to her about it to ensure she was content with me being a part of her life full-time. She said she was and anything regarding your knowing was left with Shugar to deal directly. With that being said, I will tell you a little about myself.

I am a thirty-five year old Hedge Fund Manager in New York where I work at the Stock Exchange. My parents are from Nigeria but I was born and raised in Harlem and I have no children nor have I ever been married. Finally, I'm in love with Cherisse Brown and want nothing more than for your daughter to be a permanent part of my life and for Shugar to except this proposal and become my bride."

Oh my God! Nasir just proposed! Right here. Right now. In front of Rick in my living room, he asked me to be his bride. Is he serious?

Rick's mouth is opened and he is stunned by what just

happened as I am. I didn't even notice the blue Tiffany box Nasir was displaying in front of me before I heard Rick gasp for air at the sight of the box and engagement ring.

"Cherisse Shugar Brown…. Will you marry me?" Nasir was holding my right hand and putting this gorgeous princess cut two and half carat diamond ring on my left hand. I'm in absolute amazement but I answered.

"Yes!"

Rick slammed the door behind him as he exited and I was shaken, by the force of the door closing, out of my trance. The ring fit perfectly and I was without words.

Someone wants to marry me. Me! Shugar Brown. Nasir Carlisle wants me to be his bride and right now, nothing else makes better sense.

Tonight, I'm going to make love to this man like I had never done with another human being. In spite of the pain, I will make sure he loves it and me more by the end. I plan to put it on him tonight. But first, I call Rick on his cell phone knowing he won't answer. Regardless, I leave him a message that he shouldn't bring Stormy home until late Sunday evening as opposed to early in the morning; I needed to spend quality time with my new fiancé.

NOVEMBER 21, 1998

Time: 6:09 am   Mood: Somber

Dear Shugar,

What's up Shugar? I hope this letter finds you in good health and happy. I am writing to you again knowing you won't write me back again but that's okay. At least you not sending my letters back to the prison like some dudes here. Anyway, I wanted to tell you that my parole was approved and I should be going to the half-way house in Newark in about six weeks. After I do 3 months in the half-way house, I will move back into my mother's apartment. My Grandma been paying the rent the whole time since my Mom died so at least I will have a place to rest my head. But I also wanted to talk to you about something I need help with when I get home and I hope you will be able to help me. It's about some kind of insurance policy that my father had on him and my mom. I know you work in an office and can probably help me understand what I'm supposed to do. Anyway. Talk to you later. Xo – Ibin.

12 JOURNAL ENTRY
February 2, 1999

It's groundhogs day and that Punxsutawney Phil critter climbed out of his little hole and did not see his shadow. At least he says that spring is coming early and that petite bit of news makes me feel a slight bit better; a little less nervous. This means that on my wedding day, Saturday, March 27th, I'm expecting it to be warm and sunny. A good day to get married I'd say.

Regardless of such a wonderful thought, it doesn't change the fact that in a couple of hours I'll be standing face-to-face with Ibin again finally after almost a year.

I've ignored almost every letter he has written me and only spoke to him briefly over the phone when he moved into the half-way house once in all this time. Now, I'm putting on my makeup with shaky hands edgy about telling him in person that I'm getting married. Problem is, I'm not all that sure why I feel this way. It's not like he's my man or anything or that he can say one thing to change my mind. But whatever. He asked to meet so he can show me these paper regarding his parent's insurance policy.

"So, what these insurance policies are saying is

basically that you are the sole beneficiary of both your parent's policies and are due to receive twenty-five thousand a piece off both policies. You understand?" Ibin is starting at the papers in my hand with a blank face and I can tell he is struggling to comprehend all that I am explaining and what it means to him.

"Are you telling me that I'm gonna get fifty-thousand dollars cause both my parents died?" Ibin replied.

"Well, you have to file the paperwork and confirm everything with a lawyer and the insurance company but, yes. It means you will get fifty-thousand dollars from the insurance policies your father had on himself and your mother in case of their untimely deaths." I was happy for Ibin. Getting this money would mean he would have a chance to change his life around and it will provide a second chance to do things different.

"And what about my grandma Shugar? Does she get anything?" I can tell Ibin had more questions than answers as he was also planning the future for himself and his much-loved grandmother.

"Unfortunately, your parents named you as the sole beneficiary on both of their policies and did not include your grandmother but that doesn't mean you can't do or give her whatever you want too." I explained further.

Ibin is starting to grin that odd grin of his when he is deep in thought about something that makes him super happy and I can't help but grin at his obvious happiness. Then I realized it was a great opportunity, while he was in a good mood to tell him about the wedding and my impending marriage.

"Ibin. I'm glad we got to hang out today because I

wanted to see for myself that you were okay after being away for so long and losing your mom in the process. Plus….. I wanted to tell you something face-to-face before you heard it on the streets if you haven't already." I closed my eyes and took a deep inhale while formulating my next sentence.

"You are getting married." Ibin said to me as he took my hands. I opened up one eye to peek at the look on his face and then the other but to my surprise, he was calm and he still looked like he was in a good mood.

"Yeah. That's what I was gonna say. Ummm… how did you know?"

"The streets talk and besides, last time I spoke to Jamil, he told me. Said you were planning a big fancy wedding too."

I decided to exhale and relax in the notion that Ibin wasn't hurt by the news considering that he's confessed that he had a crush on me and all.

"I don't know about fancy but it should be very nice." I turned towards Ibin and touched his leg to signal that I needed him to look me in the eyes so that I can keep an eye on his emotions during this conversation.

"I'm happy for you Shugar. You are going to make a pretty bride. Did you pick out your dress yet?" he asked with a half-smile now.

"As a matter of fact, I'm going to a bridal shop as soon as I leave you to try on a few gowns and maybe find something I love." I replied dauntingly.

"Your Mom and sister and them not going with you? Ain't that supposed to be something that you do with those people around?" Ibin asked.

"Nope. I didn't ask anyone to come with me cause well…. I'm still not back one-hundred percent with my Mom yet and really, I didn't think to ask anyone else to come with me. I figured it wouldn't be that hard to do."

Ibin looked a little concerned at my idea to go alone and offered to come. Again, I was stunned at his suggestion but I figured because he was taking the news so well, then he must be over his crush and it should be fine if he tags along to keep me company.

We arrived at the bridal shop on time for my appointment and I immediately became overwhelmed with the variety of gowns and wedding attire everywhere. My thoughts were all over the place and I pondered how I was supposed to pick out the perfect dress without the help of my only sister or any of my friends.

After I was measured and explained the style of gowns I had in mind I sat down in the dressing area awaiting the parade of dresses to begin. I had finally realized that Ibin was no longer sitting near me but was instead wondering around the store. Maybe the idea of me getting married was too much for him after all I was thinking. At that point, I had decided to not call him over when I tried on dresses to get his opinion.

I tried on the first princess styled dress that was big, frilly and just way too much for my liking. I felt like a cake topper and not a bride. The second and third gowns were more of the same and I had to explain further to my consultant that I was looking for something more old Hollywood and sexy.

Jean, the bridal consultant, ran off to look for the dress of my dreams and I was beginning to panic that I wouldn't find anything when in walked Ibin with an off-white gown carefully draped over his arm.

"Try this one on Shugar. I think you would like nice in this one."

I took the dress from his hand with a very questionable look on my own face now. "Where were you all this time? I thought you started to feel some kind of way and went to sit in the car or something."

"Just try on the gown Ms. Brown please. I think you will look nice in it." Was Ibin's only response.

Five minutes later I exited my dressing room to see the dress in the four way mirror in the family waiting area. As I stepped up on the podium and took my first spin in the mirror, I noticed Ibin sitting in the chair where my mother would be waiting patiently.

"You are beautiful Shugar." He whispered in my direction. I looked over at him and he had a look on his face I hadn't witnessed before. I had no words to describe the look except that his eyes looked like they were dancing somehow.

I had to admit that the gown, draping my body is a perfect fit, felt every bit of the glamour and sexy I was going for. Jean noticed mine and Ibin's admiration for the dress and had made the decision to help seal the deal by pinning a small veil in my hair that draped softly across my face. Stunning. I cried at my own image. This was my dress and Ibin chose it for me.

13 JOURNAL ENTRY
March 27, 1999

TODAY IS MY WEDDING DAY! And I can't be more
ecstatic, nervous and ridiculously happy all at the same time.
Stormy and I woke up to a beautiful breakfast in bed
arranged especially for us by my soon to be husband, Nasir.

I first noticed the aroma of sweet bread baking as I was
awaking out of my slumber only to notice that my baby was
comfortably still asleep in the same bed I thought I was just
sharing with Nas the night before. Apparently he had gotten
up and left the house before the crack of dawn to finish a few
wedding day errands himself or at least that is what the note
says that he left on his pillow for me to find. Along with a
dozen red roses for me and yellow roses for Stormy was an
envelope that contained a gift certificate to a day spa for me
and one hundred dollar bill to leave as a tip. What a beautiful
gesture to help me prepare for the most important day of my
life, I thought. And the spa will do everything for me; a
relaxing stone massage, facial, mani/pedi, hair and makeup.
This is great because the wedding ceremony isn't slated to

start until six o'clock in the evening as a candlelight wedding which means I have all day to relax and prepare for that magical walk down the aisle.

I wake Stormy up from her sleep and while she is finishing her breakfast, I check her overnight bag again to ensure that everything she needs to stay the weekend with Rick's parents were provided for. Rick's mother had volunteered to keep my baby while Nasir and I enjoyed our honeymoon in Hawaii. Which means that after I get my little miss bathed and primped, I can drop her off to my mother's where my sister Kyra will ensure she is dressed and ready for the wedding? Following the ceremony, Kyra will drop Stormy off to her grandparents' home and her father will check in on her.

In the interim, Rick is still pretty disgusted that I had actually gotten over him and appeared to moving on in life without so much as a ounce of regard for him. Hence why he pretended to be busy with some fake plans he and Trina supposedly have that won't allow him the opportunity to take care of his own child on the very weekend I get married. Whatever. I've worked it out with his parents so oh well. He'll get over it or he won't. I honestly don't care.

Just as I reach the day spa and announce my arrival for my pre-arranged appointment I am alerted that I have an urgent phone call from my sister and I rush to the phone.

"Hello. Kyra? What's wrong with Stormy?" I ask with urgency.   "Nothing is wrong with Stormy Shugar. Calm down. But there is something else going on down around here that you should know about." Kyra explains.

"What could possibly be going on around there on my wedding day in your neighborhood that I need to be concerned with?" I laughed a sigh of relief as I waited on what was bound to be a comical reply from my sister.

"Sister!" Kyra practically yelled into the phone to regain my attention.

"Your boy Ibin is outside sitting on the curb drunk as hell early this morning, telling anybody that want to hear it, how he is going to fuck up your wedding at the church. And Girl, he sound like he serious as hell."

"What?" I'm shocked and immediately pissed at this new revelation. I thought Ibin was fine with me getting married. After all, over the last two weeks he had gone with me virtually everywhere to finalize arrangements and purchase last minute items for the wedding. He seemed happy to do it and I was thrilled that I had someone who was becoming a close friend, to do it with. Hell. It was him who chose my wedding gown and suggested on lingerie I should where when Nas and I were alone again following the nuptials. I am wondering now why the change of heart or mind with him. What is this about, I'm left to wonder.

'Yes! And I wouldn't even bother you with this if the whole damn hood wasn't down here starting to whisper about it and gassing Ibin up more, ya know? I mean, I know you didn't even invite him but still I don't want you to be embarrassed on your day." Kyra sound like she was really concerned.

I'm thinking to only way to avoid any kind of craziness or embarrassment was to confront Ibin about it and get him to calm down.

"Do me a favor Sister. Go outside and tell Ibin in private that I'm on my way down there to see him okay?"

Okay Shugar. I'll tell him." Was Kyra's reply before we

hung up.

I turned back to the receptionist and apologized for having to push my appointment back further in the day. I explained that I had an a wedding day emergency to handle but that I would return as soon as I could to get whatever services that are still available. The receptionist said he understood and handed me a card to call the spa when I knew about what time I could return.

Next I rushed to my car and sped to my mother's neighborhood as fast as I could hoping to resolve whatever issues Ibin was having in a decent amount of time to return to the spa and allot enough time following to get dressed and arrive at the church on time.

As I was parking my car in front of my mother's home, I noticed Ibin sitting on his porch with two of his cronies along with three open bottles of what looked like Gin. I slammed my car door in furor and made my way across the street and the stairs to his house.

"I need to talk to Ibin alone please." I said that to no one in particular as I was staring at whom I considered enemy number one at this moment.

Everyone left the porch except Ibin who was looking me in the face now as he was lifting the green bottle of Tanqueray to his mouth in absolute defiance to me. He knew why I was there and was simply preparing for the battle I suppose. So I stood there for all of two minutes with my hands on my hips waiting for him to start explaining himself. But he didn't. Ibin was just staring up at me and shaking his head from side to side. His eyes were bloodshot and the strong aroma of quality marijuana was vulgar.

After a few minutes of awkward silence, I decided I

don't have time to waste waiting to get this showdown started. "So, I heard you plan to attend my wedding uninvited." I said in a very controlled voice between clinched teeth.

He puts the bottle and blunt down on the steps and stands on the step above mine so that he is looking down on me. "You getting married Shugar. You getting married today and it's not to me. Yo. I'm trippin right?"

"Ibin. You cannot be serious. You knew I was getting married and today you decide you feel some kind of way about it? For real? You've been with me for the past two weeks preparing for this day and now you telling everybody you gonna stop my wedding. I mean, the whole damn neighborhood talking about you and me like we been fucking all this time and I'm doing you dirty by marrying somebody else. You knew I was seeing Nasir and it's not like you wasn't seeing other chicks... We are not in a relationship. So why are you acting like this?" I can't hold back my anger for him right now. But he responds like he hadn't heard a word I just said.

On perfect cue Ibin replies, "I don't understand though Shugar. I mean, it's not like I didn't know you was serious about this suit and tie dude. Shit I called myself being serious about the bitch I was seeing but you know what this is. You know what it was with me and you Shugar. You marrying this niggah cause he can give you anything you want but I know you want more. Don't you? Don't you want more Cherise?"

This man has totally lost it, I'm thinking. He is being irrational and not even taking into account anything I'm saying to him. He talking to me but he's not talking to me really. Regardless, I have to fix this mess and convince him that if he attempts to ruin my wedding, he will be sorry. I'm gonna try a softer approach. I sit on the top stair and takes Ibin's hands and guides him down next to me.

"Ibin. I'm asking you to not do this to me okay? I am happy with him and this is what I want. And you are right. I do want more and I think I'm going to have more with Nasir. He loves me Ibin. He loves me and I love him and we are getting married today. I know you have this crush on me but if you care about me at all you won't do anything to hurt me." I'm hoping this last comment seals the deal and changes his mind about doing anything stupid.

"Listen." Ibin says as he places both hands on either side of my face.

"I'm not going to fuck up your wedding Shugar. I'm just talking shit cause I'm in pain that's all. And yeah, I'm real fucked up in the head right now but I love you too much to do anything that will hurt you in any way. So you don't need to worry about me coming down to the church to fuck shit up. Okay? But I want to tell you something while you still Miss Brown. You know I love you and even though you don't want to admit it to yourself, you got some kind of feelings for me too. You may not be in love with me but what me and you got... Man! It ain't no words for it except plain love. And you can keep telling yourself that you're all happy and shit with ole' boy but you know that I know what's up. So go head and get married Shorty. Stand up there and say them vows knowing you supposed to be with me."

With that, Ibin stands up again and walks into his house, shuts and locks the door, leaving me standing on the porch with a confused look on my face. At least I don't have to worry about him embarrassing me at the church later. I feel bad that he is hurting behind all this but I can't waste any more time trying to make him feel comfortable about the situation. Besides, he said he was fine so fine.

I decided to go over to my mother's house to see how they were all getting along before calling the Spa and heading back that way. As I entered the house, my mother was in her robe, smoking a cigarette with rollers in her head. She seemed surprised to see me as I approached her.

"What you doing here Shugar? Shouldn't be somewhere getting your head done or something?" Sheila asks me as me as my sister and brother Ethan both enter the living room area.

"Yep. And I'm on my way there now actually. I just wanted to drop in and make sure you didn't need anything for Stormy to get her ready." I replied to my mother as Kyra was shooting me the 'I hope you handled your handle' look. My mother didn't reply in return. Instead, she disappeared up the stairs and yelled at my daughter about putting toys in the bathwater she had prepared.

Kyra grabs me by the hand and pulls me into the laundry room to ask if I had indeed put out the fire with Ibin and I assured her I had. Following our brief conversation, I made my way back outside, into my car and back home to relax. I decided I wasn't in the mood to be pampered after all and I would just do my own hair and makeup instead. I had no real reason for the sudden somber mood I was in but I thought it best to just be alone and work on putting on a happy face before saying I Do to Mr. Nasir Carlisle.

The wedding was beautiful and without interruption

from anyone. Both our families enjoyed the festivities and Ethan took great pride in giving me away.

Taking our family portraits was a lot of fun. First, I took a few very nice intimate photos with just Stormy and myself and then with Nasir, Stormy and I; a new blended family.

Following a few other pictures taken, the photographer called on all the family members of both families to take one large group picture on the church steps.

My sister Kyra was just over my head and my mother was at my right side. When she noticed a strange face climb the steps to insert himself in the picture, she whispered over her shoulder to me and gestured to Kyra to listen in.

"Who is that guy with the lavender tie getting in the picture? Is he related to your husband?"

"No. I've met all of Nasir's guests but he do look a little familiar." I whispered back.

"Do you know who he is Kyra?"

"No but he giving me the creeps. Looking all shifty eyed and grinning like the Cheshire cat from Alice in Wonderland."

My mother, Kyra and I all laughed at her last comment. Just then, my grandmother Mary leaned in and said, "If I didn't know better, I'd swear that man was Stormy's Daddy! She can just about pass for his twin; same eyes, dirty blonde curly hair and all...."

The three of us stopped giggling at that comment and stared straight ahead as we heard click after click of the camera. We dared not say another word about it but we were all thinking the same thing. And that thought wasn't pleasant or amusing at all. But we weren't going to acknowledge Grandmother Mary's remark either for the fear that she'd keep gabbing about it.

Otherwise, nothing seemed out of place during the ceremony or reception but I couldn't bring myself to understand why the man in the lavender tie looked so familiar or why the thought of him kept me from being at a ten with excitement.

After saying our goodbyes to everyone and Stormy, Nasir and I left for our honeymoon that night and spent the next eight days in marital bliss. Yet somehow, and I couldn't put my finger on why, I never got back to a abundantly happy me. Disturbing.

14 JOURNAL ENTRY
December 27, 1999

I quietly opened Stormy's door and walked to her bedside to wake her and get her ready for a week off from school with her grandparents. Their Christmas gift to her was a week -long trip to Disneyland with just the two of them and I know she couldn't wait to be on her way.

She was sound asleep still, lying on her side facing the window. Even in her slumber, she was drawn to the sunlight like a sun dial. I leaned over her bed to let the shade all the way up when I noticed there were roller pins on her night table. About a dozen of them and a few had long tresses of hair still attached as if they had broken off with the uncurling of someone's hair.

When I go to investigate it closer, Stormy stirs out of her sleep, turns or her back and smiles a big smile at me. I put the thought of the pins on the back burner for now.

"Is it time to go to Disneyland Mommy?"

"Yep! Sure is, but you have to get washed up and dressed before Nanna and Pop-Pop get here. Can you do that by yourself?"

She shakes her messy bed hair from side-to-side and

climbs out of bed.

When she is safely out the door and knowingly gone from my presence for a week I find my new husband in the master bedroom lacing his winged tipped shoes and grabbing his keys.

"Hey you. I thought you took the day off and we were spending time together. I wanted to try on those crotchless edible panties for you Husband." I pouted when I noticed he was planning to leave the house.

"Yeah I know, but a huge deal just became available that I have to jump on while it's still hot. You understand don't you?"

Nasir was charming and smooth with his words but I realized fairly quickly that nothing I was going to say would change his mind. So, I decided I had nothing to lose in asking...

"Real quick. During the Christmas get together with your family, did you notice if anyone came in or out of Stormy's room? I had forbidden her from having company in there just because I wanted her to play in her play area and not tear that room apart."

"Ummm. No. Why?" Nasir asked with his eyebrows furled at me.

"Because I found hair roller pins on her night table. I don't wear rollers or use hair pins and neither does Stormy so I thought it was odd. Like maybe someone from the get together had come into her room for something."

Then a thought surged through my brain with 'SPECIAL DELIVERY' stamped all over it.

"But now that I think about it.... She and I cleaned that room yesterday morning before we left for church. And I remember that especially because she had called me to come and clean up after she had made a huge mess with that Elmer's glue and glitter kit someone gave her and those pins weren't there then. And the party was a couple of days ago."

Nasir kissed me on the lips and quietly said, "Stop buggin' out. It's nothing. Throw them in the garbage and be done with it. You're right. One of my cousins probably did come in here to use the phone or something and took the pins out of their head. Who cares?" He was so blasé about it.

As he rushed out the door, the house phone rang and it was his friend Darren from work, asking if Nasir still wanted the ride to the city since his car was in the shop.

I became more interested in what was going on because Nasir's car wasn't in the shop. He just drove off in his car. Why would he tell Darren that.

After pondering for a few more minutes, I thought it best to keep it to myself. I did tell Darren that Nas had left earlier however, in his own car.

Because the house is quiet after days of Christmas celebrations, I think it's a good idea to wash all the linens in the house while on vacation from work.

As I pull the pillow covers from Stormy's bed, I notice there are two smeared lipstick stains and a broken acrylic nail underneath the sheet in the corner of the bed. What the fuck, I think.

I picked up the pillow case and broken nail and examined each carefully. That's when I noticed the small semen stains and the distinct aroma of Passion perfume by Elizabeth Taylor on the sheets.

Now that's some grown woman shit which means there

was another adult woman in my house in my daughters bed FUCKING!

Feeling disgusted that my daughter has slept in a bed where someone else had sex was sending me over the edge. I stripped her mattress bare and stuffed it all into garbage bags to be disposed of. There was no way that shit was staying in my house.

Curiously, I ran to my bedroom and pulled Nasir's shirt from the hamper. The one he had worn yesterday and sure enough, it smelled like Passion.

That no good motherfucker had someone in my house, in my daughter's bed!

I felt my nerves unraveling and decided to drive to the coffee shop one town over to retrieve an extra-large cup of their caramel flavored coffee. The owner always took my order and would add other flavors to make my java to taste a lot like a melted Almond Joy. I was craving that kind of luxury right now.

As I climb back into my own car and begin to exit the parking lot, I thought I saw Nasir's car leave out the opposite end of the parking lot with a female passenger. I doubled back in but the car I thought was his had already entered the highway and well on the way to wherever. Was that Nasir?

15 JOURNAL ENTRY
December 27, 1999

Before I was married, I had this grand idea in my head what it would mean for me and my daughter. In my dreams, I'd live like a suburban queen so to speak. Working a part-time office job would only be necessary to use the paychecks for 'spending money' while my daughter went to the best private school in whatever state I was living. I'd live in a huge house and drive only the top of the line cars like BMWs, Mercedes and Lexus'. My husband would be my equal and be every bit the protector I'd need him to be to feel safe and comfortable.

When I imagined my life as a wife, my husband was faithful to a fault and he wanted for nothing from me. He would be sexed on a regular; morning noon and night in spite of how much it hurt me physically. I had every intention of being the well-respected social butterfly who was invited to all the best events while being his sideline whore in the bedroom. If he wanted it, I was going to ensure he got it. Hand jobs, blow jobs, oral and anal sex were all going to be his options whenever he so chose. Nine months later, I'm forced to still be daydreaming.

Nasir is a good man with great potential except I'm starting to realize, he isn't the man for me for so many reasons. Don't get me wrong. The first few months with him were incredible! He was very attentive to my needs and wants sexually and otherwise. Nasir came home every night before seven o'clock and he cooked on weekends. We had regular date nights with just the two of us and then we had one night a week that was just about myself, Nasir and of course Stormy. I couldn't ask for a better step-dad for her. He took care of us and treated her as if she was his alone. I loved that she loved him as much as it appeared he loved her.

But then things started happening and everything began to change. After the six or seventh month, my loving husband was growing distant and cold towards me and my daughter. Nasir started coming home later and later and then some nights, not at all. He stopped making sexual advances towards me and eventually, sex became non-existent all together unless I initiated it. And to do that I always had to wait until he was sound asleep and then arouse him awake with a blow job. Approaching him this way was my only guarantee that he'd be delighted and too excited to turn me down; otherwise, he'd reject me.

I found myself having to do other tricks too just to keep him interested long enough to ensure I'd get my rocks off. Otherwise, Nasir Carlisle was not at all interested in Mrs. Cherise Carlisle.

However, I knew our relationship was coming to a

definite end the morning I arrived at my office to listen to a voicemail message from a Gabrielle Washington. She said she needed to speak to me urgently regarding my husband and that I would want to hear what she had to say. Miss Gabrielle left a home number for me to return her call. I did; promptly from my desk.

She didn't come off as most women who know that have one up on you when they've been fucking your husband behind your back. What she explained to me in full detail was that she and Nasir had been seeing each for well over five months after meeting at a conference for brokers in Atlanta Georgia.

Apparently, their relationship started off with frequent hotel visits during the day in the City while my husband was supposed to be at work. Over the course of their meet-ups, Nas told her all about me and Stormy and how although he adored us, the fact that I was raped and suffered from what he called Post Traumatic Stress Disorder, he was finding it hard to deal with. My frequent nightmares were becoming an issue for him and the on-going back and forth with my daughter's father were supposed to be the root of his issues. Not to mention, he told her that the ugly scars and permanent bruises on my legs, breasts and vagina disgusted him and he didn't think I was capable of giving him the son he one day hoped to have.

Gabrielle also told me that she had been to my house several times and fucked my husband in our marital bed more than once. Can you believe that Nasir could be so disrespectful to me? I was floored.

At the end of our conversation, she revealed that she was now pregnant herself and although she knew that the relationship she carried on with my husband was wrong in every way, she had fallen in love with him and had no intentions of walking away from their relationship. Gabrielle wanted me to know that she and Nasir had recently bought a house together in Connecticut and they planned on being a family permanently. After he divorced me of course.

Her only reason for contacting me was that Nasir had promised to break the news to me and move in with her before the baby was born and he hadn't done that yet. She was becoming increasingly concerned that he wouldn't ever do it considering the fact that he once told her he felt sorry for me and my daughter and even though he wasn't in-love with me anymore, he never wanted to hurt me.

Soon after my conversation with Gabrielle had ended, I found myself in the ladies room flushing my breakfast down the toilet. I was so sick to my stomach from the thought of the betrayal my husband had served me by way of Gabrielle Washington, it was all I could stand to keep from pulling my hair out strand-by-strand.

That evening, when Nasir finally arrived home, he found most of his belongings stacked neatly in the garage of our two story neo-eclectic styled home in Livingston, New Jersey. The locksmith was just packing his tools back inside his truck after changing all the doors and installing a new alarm system on all the windows when my husband had pulled into the driveway.

I was waiting in the door for Nasir to address me about what was happening but he wore a look like he understood completely what was occurring and why. He asked if he could say goodbye to Stormy and I quietly shook my head "no". He excepted that and began to stack as many boxes as he could in the backseat and trunk of his car.

When it was realized he couldn't fit another thing, he turned to me again and simply said, "I'm sorry Shugar."

I shut and locked the door and laid in the foyer of my home for three days crying and asking God why. I never got an answer.

16 JOURNAL ENTRY
February 14, 2000

What can I say? When it rains it pours in my life. After filing for my impending divorce and having to find new affordable living quarters for me and my daughter, I then found myself in the throes of dealing with death.

When my sister Kyra called me early that Wednesday morning to say that Mommy didn't wake up that morning and that I should meet them at the hospital, I felt like my world came to an instant halt. I mean, as much as my mother and I were not on the best of terms, she was still one of the most important people in my life. The thought of her not being around for me or Stormy ever again was unimaginable.

I had made it from my home to University Hospital in twenty minutes flat before I was out of my car and in the emergency room looking for any signs of my family. I saw Kyra first. She was at the counter filling out paperwork on behalf of our mother when I approached her. I can tell by the way her hands were shaking and her eyes were darting from left to right that she was not in control of her own thoughts. I put my right hand around her upper body and took the unstable pen out of her fingers while hugging her all at the same time. Without words I was attempting to express that I will handle the paperwork and she should sit down and try to calm herself a little.

Shortly thereafter, my brother Ethan came dashing in followed behind Jamal and my uncle James. Kyra was explaining to all of us how the night before Mommy had ate an entire box of Dunkin Donuts by herself and gulped down a large iced tea along with it. After she was done with that, she sent Kyra to the store for her third pack of cigarettes that day which she proceeded to smoke one behind the other. Mom went to bed early that night complaining of exhaustion and a stomach ache but Kyra thought nothing of it considering what she had witnessed earlier. Except the next morning when my Mom is usually up and on her way to work around 6:30 am, she was still in her bed thought to be sound asleep.

Kyra went on to say how after she herself was leaving for work and Mommy still wasn't out of her bed or awake at all she had gotten so concerned that she went in and noticed that her eyes had rolled in her head and her breathing was shallow. My sister called an ambulance and after working on my mother inside the house for a few minutes, it was told to Kyra that my mother's blood sugar had shot up so high that she was in a diabetic coma.

The first night my mother was admitted, we were all in a state of shock and disarray. It was the first time ever that our mother, the fearless leader of our family, was not leading us. We were not sure how to react to that emotion.

I was numb. I walked into her room and saw her so

helpless with the tubes and machines all attached to her body and it took my breath away. In that moment I realized I wasn't done with her yet. I still needed her. I still wanted her to love and accept me for who I was. I still needed my mother to be proud of me for once.

That Friday morning, I decided to distract myself and take myself to work and Stormy to school. I had made arrangement with Rick to pick her up from school and keep her on my weekend so that I can concentrate on preparing my mother's home for her return that I had determined would be very soon.

I was getting my office and desk in order after being out for two days so I was returning phone messages and replying to emails left for me when my caller-id was informing me that my brother Ethan was calling from his cell phone. I thought that was odd considering he told me he would be at Mommy's house until noon before leaving to meet with her doctor's about her condition.

"Good morning. This is Cherise. Ethan? What's wrong?" Is how I answered the phone.

"Mommy's doctor's wants us to come to the hospital right away." Ethan was talking fast and breathing heavy. I knew instantly, this wasn't good. But before I could ask a question, he had hung up the phone.

Next, I informed my manager that I had another family emergency and needed to leave the office right away. My manager, Stacey, was very concerned with me in that moment as I explained that something was going on with my mom and she offered to drive me herself. As I grabbed my purse and was dialing my sister's number to make sure she was on her well as well, I had this overwhelming feeling of my spirit being separated from my body. I can't describe it any better than that but it felt like I was being torn into two people and that feeling stopped me cold.

I looked over at my manager and said quietly, without a whimper in my own voice, "my mother just passed away." Stacey took my hand in hers and pulled me into a strong embrace.

Walking into the hospital and into her room, seeing my mother lay so still on that bed was heavy on my heart. I couldn't cry still but I needed to and I was becoming aggravated that I hadn't cried like everyone else yet. But I climbed in the bed with my Mommy and put her arm around me as I curled up to her still warm body one last time. My only thought was that she was gone before we could fix it. Before we could fix us.

The final hours with my mother above ground were of no comfort still. I had yet to shed a tear although I was very quiet and kept to myself a lot. I stood behind my Uncle James at the cemetery when my mother's Pastor was giving her the last rites and people were tossing roses on her casket as it stood suspended over the hole in the earth. When the grave workers began to lower my mother in the ground, my sister Kyra cried out such a gut wrenching curdled cry, I could no longer hold onto the ache inside me. I lurched away and began to scream as hard and as loud as my voice would allow.

Uncle James thought, for some reason, it would lessen my pain or help me get some kind of closure if I came closer to the hole to witness them bury her beneath the ground we were all standing on so he took me by the arm and attempted to lead me nearer. I jerked away from him and told him I didn't want to see that but he insisted. I walked away from him but he followed me still telling me I needed to see it. Why? I thought. I wanted so desperately to get away from him that I was practically running with him in hot pursuit of me.

Finally, someone had pulled me into their arms to protect me from my uncle and it didn't matter who as long as I didn't have to keep running from him. I found complete solace in whoever's chest I was heaving. This person felt strong enough to hold me up if need be.

As I began to calm down, I heard first my brother Ethan call my name and then attempt to pull me away from the stranger's chest I had buried my face and then my husband Nasir made the same effort only to have this person; now my guardian tell them both no. When my sister Kyra came over to tell me that Rick was taking my daughter with him to the repast I decided I needed to give my new protector back their personal space and pull myself together. I pulled away and looked up at my protector and realized it was Ibin.

After the gravesite was totally emptied of everyone who came to pay their last respects to my mom, Ibin and I found an old oak tree to sit under and talk.

"How are you holding up?" Ibin asked as I leaned against his shoulders to rest my weary body.

"As well as to be expected I suppose." I paused to wipe the new stream of tears running down my face. "I didn't expect to see you hear today Ibin. Thanks for coming."

"Of course I was going to be here for you Shugar. You were there for me when my Moms died. It's only right that I'm here for you and my man Jamil now.

After five minutes, I break the soft silence between Ibin and I. "I've missed you Ibin. How have you been?" He didn't look at me. Instead he continued to look at the grass beneath his feet. Then he lifted my hand from the soil and laced his fingers in mine while placing them both on his lap.

"Thank you for…. you know.. for protecting me from everybody earlier. I appreciate that." I was experiencing this great ache in my heart for Ibin to just look at me like he use too. Like he stilled loved me.

"Shugar, you never have to thank me for loving you. I'm always going to love you. I accept that now. And because I'm always going to love you, I'm always gonna want to protect you. It didn't matter to me today who wanted to comfort you or be near you. The only thing that mattered was that you were okay. I would have fought an army to make that a truth. But you are married and I respect that so I've kept my distance and chose to not make waves for you. No matter what though, if you need me I'ma be there."

Ibin and I sat a few more minutes in the cemetery alone and without words. I found myself cradled under his arms or squeezing his hands tight through the pains shooting through my heart. Finally when I felt calm enough, I threw one last rose on top of my mother's casket and I followed Ibin back to his SUV. He drove me to my Mother's house and dropped me off at the front door. I didn't see or hear from him again for another three months.

17 JOURNAL ENTRY
May 30, 2000

It's funny how the most simple of things can trigger a memory. A certain scent or a song on the radio. Someone could speak a sentence in a manner that opens flood gates of memoirs for self.

Since Ethan had made the decision on all of our behalf to sell Mommy's house, I was assigned her room to rummage through and pack. All of us, Kyra, Jamal, Ethan and I had taken different parts of our childhood home to put memories in boxes and pack away safely.

Sitting in my mother's living room, I'm on her bedroom floor surrounded by clothes, shoes and piles of envelopes and she had crushed in her closet in crates.

As I sit here I find myself smiling at the pictures of me and my siblings when we were younger and without care in the world. When Mommy was our superhero because she was unstoppable and fearless. We felt so protected by her that we never noticed that we had no father in the house. Sheila Roberts raised her boys to be men and protectors of their sisters. She instilled in Kyra and I the idea of a 'strong black woman' and taught us to never apologize for being beautiful and smart.

I came across a black and white picture of Mommy when she was nineteen years old. She was model beautiful. Eyes so big and round, they were captivating and exotic. Her smile was wide and her teeth were sparkling white. Everyone said Mommy was so smart and intelligent, even at that age, that she was sometimes a little crazy. Staring at this picture though, I can almost see a hurt that would explain her crazy. I saw me in her eyes staring back at me.

I was shocked to find that the next box was filled to the brim of pictures of me and Stormy. Pictures of Stormy when she was first born in the hospital and me looking a hot crazy mess after giving birth.

There was a 8 x 10 picture of me in the third grade. Wow! My hair was in three long pig tails; two on the sides and one great big one on top with a white yarn ribbon. I had on a ruby red dress that had an apron of sorts over it with a picture of Holly Hobbie and the words, "Life is full of little surprises. I remember that being my favorite outfit then. I wanted to wear it all the time. Underneath that picture, folded tight and wrapped in tissue paper is the apron. I can't believe she kept this.

I find the scrapbook she must have started when I was born. Her first born daughter. In it was her journal entry dated by birth day.

Today I had the honor of birthing the most beautiful thing on earth. YOU. You are the color of milk chocolate and your eyes look like little chocolate morsels. Your lips are tiny and puckered to perfection and since entering this world you haven't cried once but you are cooing and smiling a lot while reaching for me. Your Momma. I don't think I've ever been more in love with another human being. Not even your brothers. I know I shouldn't tell you that but it's true. I didn't even have the normal labor pains with you. Instead, your little fists rapped on my lower spine as if you were knocking for permission to be let into the world. And when it was time for your full arrival, I pushed once and you were here. No torturous contractions. No wild screaming and begging for drugs. Nothing. Just like that, there you were. The light in your eyes make up for all the wrongs in my life. I forgive your father for taking from me with force what I didn't offer to give. Staring into your face I know now that God gave me you as a peace treaty to make up for conceiving you in an act of violence. The sweetest thing I've ever known. Like a little brown sugar cube. It's only befitting I crown you Shugar. Cherise Shugar Brown!

The next page is my original birth certificate. Mother: Sheila Roberts. Birthplace: Martlin Hospital., Newark New Jersey Father: Kevin Brown. But there is a hand-written note underneath my father's signature. "Thank you Sheila for giving me a daughter and allowing me to share in her life and giving her my last name as if she is my own."

What hell is that supposed to mean? As if she is my own... is Kevin Brown not my father? I'm so confused. I drop that box and open another one. I find more pictures and other scrapbooks of the other children. None I've ever seen or Sheila ever shared with me and I'm sure, none of the other kids before. I check each of their birth certificates, fully expecting to different names on each for some reason. But no. All signed by Kevin Brown but no message underneath his signature.

One more box at the bottom of the closet and I rip the top off. It's filled with envelopes holding old court papers and doctor's notes about me. These papers are from the rape trial. There are papers about dates to appear in court. Instructions on what to expect. Dates scribbled on the fronts and backs of envelopes as if she was taking notes of something. There is a calendar from that year with days circled in red and notes to attend which doctor or psychiatrists on what day and time. Then I open the biggest envelope that is marked 'Discoveries" and I tear it open.

I sat on my mother's floor for another hour reading page after page of testimony from witnesses and co-defendants regarding that horrible night. When I read the name, Tyrick Monroe Marshall, I purposely went over that first sentence with Rick's name carefully.

Officer Barnes: In interviewing co-defendant Omar Wicks he stated that Tyrick (aka Rick) Monroe Marshall came by his house immediately following the attack on himself and Miss Brown to pay the debt in full. Omar Wicks also stated that he contacted Matthew (aka Bull) James to confirm that the $1,500 cash that was brought to the apartment of Wicks by Marshall was the total amount owed and that he could allow Marshall to leave the building without further incident.

The name, Bull, did not ring new to my ears. I had heard that name before but I didn't know why or where I heard it but I kept reading the pages that followed.

Officer Barnes: We brought witness Matthew (aka

Bull) James in next to interview and he confessed that he
knew about the planned robbery of Marshall and that he had
helped to plan out what was supposed to happen and in what
order with Marshall himself. However, when it was told
after the fact that Cherise was attacked and raped in the
process of the robbery instead, he threatened to call the
police. James did not contact the authorities as threatened
but when we brought in for questioning, he gave up the
names of the other parties involved who are the defendants
in court today. James also stated, and all the defendants
confirmed, that he did not take part in the robbery as planned
because his young son had a severe asthma attack earlier in
the day and he stayed home to care for him.

My mind was racing and I was developing a major
migraine in the process of reading and attempting to make
sense of what I had in my hands. None of it was making
sense really. In sorts, it sounds like Rick was set-up to be
robbed that night but then why would he take $1,500 cash to
my rapists right after the attack? And who is the "Bull"
person who helped to plan the robbery but didn't say
anything about what he knew until the cops called him for
questioning. More importantly, why didn't I know any of
this before now and why did my mother keep these papers?

I had more questions than answers at this point and I
was beginning to have a severe panic attack as memories of
those court hearings and doctor's appointments began to
flood my brain. One scene after the other.

I was replaying conversations with Rick in my head
over and over where I had asked him where he left too the
night of the rape. I wanted to know why he wasn't there in

the field when it was over. Why I didn't see or hear from him for weeks following and why he didn't come see me in the hospital. Rick had always convinced me that I was in a foggy state of mind and that he was there but I had somehow blocked it out.

I was daydreaming about conversations with my mother where she was questioning me over and over about trying to remember if Rick had exchanged any words with my attackers before being dragged into the field. Or if any of them said anything to me that stood out in the course of my soul being stamped out of my body.

I had always dismissed trying to remember much of anything and I only remembered things in bits and pieces. Small flashes of their faces sweating profusely standing over me would wake me up in the middle of the night. Once when Stormy was an infant and I was changing her diaper and tickling her just to hear her giggle. I remember at one point she made this face that stopped me cold because she looked exactly like Omar Wicks. It was the grin on her face in that moment that forced a flash memory of the same crooked grin he had on his face as he was stuffing a broomstick in my vaginal cavity.

My tormentors haunted my days and my nights for decades and when they were not present in my mind, they worked quietly creating small holes in my heart. I was never without them and here they are again on full blast. Threatening my small sanity on the very day I am supposed to be putting the memories of my mother in a box forever.

Reading the pages of these discoveries along with diagrams of all the wounds that were counted on the 'victim's body I began instantly reliving the darkest day of my life. It was sort of like someone started a silent movie in my head. I'm feeling blood red inside. Sitting in this little room, I allowed the rage building inside me to finally boil to the top of my lungs and I abruptly release the full furor of ten years of absolute agony.

I stood up and began to smash the mirrors in my mother's room. I threw papers in the air and shredded piles of pictures to little pieces. My arms were flailing and knocking my mother's knick-knacks off the dressers and pulling the mattresses of the bed frame. I couldn't stop myself. I felt the arms of my brothers trying to restrain me but I was doped up on adrenaline and I was stronger than the two of them put together. Tossing them both to the side I destroyed my mother's room from corner to corner; ceiling to floor.

I was talking to my mother out loud telling her that she'd hated me since I was raped, that I didn't deserve the things she'd said to me or about me. I told her that she stopped loving me and so I couldn't heal from the rape. I spoke to my attackers. I told them they stole my life and left me broken. That I didn't do enough in my life to justify living with nightmares night after night. Everything I'd ever felt or thought—even things I hadn't been aware of—came out.

I found the small razor blades my mother kept on her night stand, always in an otherwise empty Newport box. She kept it there for protection in case someone ever entered her room uninvited and with danger on their mind. But I was going to use it to bring much needed relief to myself.

Living didn't seem like an option in this hour. With each cut I felt the surging of the pain begin to drain from my body and that's okay. It was time to stop all the lies to myself about everything I ever told myself about my own life being good. It was an absolute disaster and any choices to change the direction I was heading would all lead me back to this road, so why not.

After a few minutes of bleeding profusely, I'm aware that I'm dying. It feels good to experience such hurt and misery leave the space where your heart was supposed to dwell alone. The area where my heart was supposed to live in peace was crammed tight. It's too small to share the space with a soul that is so full of negativity. Letting go has become a liberation. I feel light... like I'm floating.

Death isn't supposed to be like this. Where is the *nothing*? At this stage, I'm supposed to have wings and wearing a long white robe, hovering over my loved ones as they grieve me.

I kept waiting for the darkness; for my consciousness to shut down completely but it never came. My sense of self remained relevant and I was disappointed at my confusion.

Confusion meant I was still breathing, albeit with labored breath, but still alive nonetheless.

When I collapsed to the floor, I was done. I felt empty of any true feelings and exhausted.

Ethan, Kyra and Jamal were standing in the doorway in shell shock and I knew that they would never again look at me as being in control or fully sane. But in a strange way, before the paramedics had arrived, I did sense that something had died, if not my whole self.

I sat crying for what felt like hours but was only minutes, in the piles of mess I had created, as if I were in mourning. The color of self-hate, thick and slow, running down my arms, creating a vibrant red sea on the floor surrounding me. My energy source, my fight, the rage that had moved me to lose my mind in those instances —it was all at the surface now. I felt the blood rushing through my body like a heat wave.

Finally I had blacked out from blood loss and pure exhaustion of the mind body and spirit.

18 JOURNAL ENTRY
June 5, 2000

I didn't hurt. I'm thinking that I should probably be in some kind of pain -- but I'm not. I'm not particularly a huge fan of pain so it being absent from my body was fine by me.

Apparently, I'm still alive. Everything appears to be distant and unreal and I know I should be trying to get up from this bed. That I should be urgently trying to find out where my daughter was and who was taking care of her. But I had no real desire to move in such a groggy state of being.

I notice my head feels like it's ten sizes too big for my shoulders. I feel dizzy; even with my eyes closed. I went to unglue my eyes with the ball of my fists but I couldn't move my arms. My wrists are moving and the muscles are working but I cannot lift my limbs from my sides. Strange. Suddenly I was discerned that my ankles are strapped down too. I hear voices talking around my head I decide to force my eyes open slowly.

Ethan and his wife Tasha are arguing over the flowers in the corner of the room being too big or too small an arrangement. But I smell a familiar fragrance in the room. It smells like butterscotch and brown sugar.

"Mommy you're woke!" It's the face of my nine year old angel. Stormy jumps up on the bed and wraps her arms around my neck and squeeze so tight I gasp for air. Tasha pulls her off me and orders her onto the floor and she obeys with pouted lips but no back talk.

I try to speak but my mouth is so dry and pasty. Ethan took notice and puts a cup of to my mouth to sip water from a straw.

"Hey Sis! How you feel?" My brother is looking at me with questionable eyes and I'm staring right back attempting to get my baring about me.

Woozily I answer, "I'm okay. What's going on? Why am I strapped to the bed?"

Tasha sits on the bed near my chest and leans in towards my face as if she had a secret to tell me.

"Shugar. You are in the hospital Sweetie. You've been here for almost a week now. The doctors have kept you heavily sedated." Tasha voice trailed off and I followed her eyes as she looked up to my brother to finish the thought she was having.

"You had a nervous breakdown." Ethan blurted that out and dropped his eyes to floor. He was ashamed of what he telling me. Either that or he felt guilty to deliver what he assumed was such terrible news.

Tasha jumped up from the bed and convinced Stormy to travel with her down a few floors to the hospital's gift shop so that they could pick out something for me. I could tell Stormy was not anxious at all to leave me so soon after I had obviously just awakened but like I said, she is a very obedient child and so she followed her aunt without giving her trouble.

Once they left the room, I locked eyes with Ethan and steered his eyes down towards the buckles on my ankles and wrists. He knew what I was asking.

"I don't know what you remember Shugar but a couple of days ago, you were packing up Mommy's room by yourself and you must have come across something that set you off because out of nowhere..... it's like you went crazy. You trashed Mommy's room and was screaming at the top of lungs. You were uncontrollable." He took my hand in his and continued.

"You cut yourself with a razors and then blacked out." He paused again to emphasize his next few sentences. "When you woke up in the hospital, you starting acting up again. Thrashing around. Throwing. Spitting. Talking to yourself and to Mommy. The doctor's thought it best to keep you partially sedated and tied down so that you don't hurt yourself."

I allowed his words to seep into my psyche and penetrate the core of me. I sat staring at my brother for what seemed like hours but was only two short minutes, recognizing the hurt and pain in his own eyes. Numberless tears stained both our faces. No sound. No further breakdown in either of our composure. My nucleus was shattered into a million teeny tiny pieces once I realized the crux of what I had done to me; to them. My family. Stormy.

"I'm sorry Ethan." I whispered as I squeezed his hands in mine.

"I don't know what is going on with me. I've been so okay with what happened for years and all of a sudden I'm starting to fall apart. I'm so sorry."

"You have nothing to be sorry for Shugar. We didn't

give you the support you needed. Mommy was wrong for not being there for you like she could have been. I'm wrong cause I'm your big brother. I left for the military cause I didn't want to deal in the misery that was happening at home. All of us should be telling you how sorry we are that you were......"

Ethan was struggling with the one word that could possibly liberate me from this iron cage I've been in. It was all I could do in that moment to force it out of him. He needed to say the word and I needed to be set free. I stayed silent in a protest to not help him help me. After all, he is my big brother and I need him to act like it in this moment.

"Listen. I have never gotten over the fact that I didn't get too you two minutes sooner to prevent those motherfuckers from ra..." He stalled again.

"THEY RAPED ME ETHAN! WHAT THE FUCK?"

I found my voice and retired from my protest. The idea that no one has said the word to me in ten fucking years forces all the tiny shattered pieces in me to come together like magnets and align themselves again. I immediately remembered I was in restraints and thought it best to calm myself.

I took a deep breath and began again. More tranquil.

"The word is rape Ethan. They raped me. And as hard as that is for me to say, it's even harder that YOU can't say it. Because it happened to me and you act like saying it or me talking about it hurts you more than it had ever hurt me. That's why I'm here. Not because those niggahs violated me but because I was never allowed to talk about it. I was forbidden to react to it. No one ever gave me permission to be sad about it. My own family never told me it wasn't my fault or even cried with me. You all pretended it didn't transpire. Like it never happened!! But you sat around and whispered. You questioned, right along with the outsiders, if Stormy is Rick's daughter or is she is a product of the rape. You all acted as if the nightmares I have are from a bad horror movie and not from a real life horror story.

Damn it. I'm strapped to this bed right now cause for years, my mother never told me I AM the product of rape Ethan. Your mother allowed me to believe that we all shared the same father but it's not true! The man who fathered me, raped her and she hated me because I am her! Life restarted. So when history repeated itself, she couldn't do a damn thing to stop the pain she knew I would endure for the rest of my life. And she knew what I'd go through....because it's what she went through.

What's worse is that she knew all along that my daughter's father may be the reason I was attacked in the first place and never uttered one word to me about it. Our mother watched me fawn after Rick. She scrutinized me for begging him to love me; needing him to acknowledge that I even existed. She deliberately kept the secret that that bastard was the source of my wounds."

Ethan was stunned by my words I can tell. I can see all the same questions I had, sitting on the floor of my mother's bedroom opening file after file, paper after paper, racing through his mind now.

"I'm not going to hurt myself Ethan. Not anymore. I have to live for my daughter. I understand that now. I'm asking you....please have them remove the restraints from me." I was pleading with him to finally be released of the shackles that have been holding me back.

A few hours later I was awakened by an urgent need to urinate and when I went to throw my legs over the bed onto the floor, I was shocked to find that my hands and feet were no longer restrained.

As I am washing my hands, I take a look at myself in the mirror and was surprised at the image staring back at me. It was Cherise and she was nineteen again. I had almost forgotten what she looked like until now. There was happiness in her eyes and in her smile. I blinked really hard and splashed water on my face to ensure what I was staring at was just my imagination. And just like that…she was gone again.

As I stared at myself now I was so disgusted with myself; with the victim I was looking at. The victim of rape, the victim of relationship abuse, victim of poor parenting, victim of young motherhood, victim of self-hate and self-doubt. VICTIM. I was so unsure of what needed to happen next so I stared at myself for a long while. Finally the thought came to me to change that reflection in the mirror to a new me. Right then and there, I had decided on a new normal; whatever that meant. The proposal of a new me made me take notice of the hard thumping in my chest. The rhythm of my heartbeat became apparent to me for the first time ever. Knowing in that moment, I would work on that woman in the mirror as soon as I got home.

I stepped out of the bathroom to hear Rick knocking on my door with a huge balloon arrangement and two dozen yellow roses. I pushed passed him and made my way back into the bed where I pulled the covers tight to my chin and sunk all the way down until I was laying flat on my back again. I wasn't ready to deal with him. Partly because I still didn't understand what part he played if any in the rape. I needed to investigate that fact a little further and find out who 'Bull' was that seems to be at the root of the happenstance. Until then, I needed to play coy and act distant.

"Hey Beautiful!" Rick exclaimed as he leaned down to kiss my cheek of which I offered gingerly.

"I saw your brother Ethan downstairs. He said you wasn't up for any more visitors today but I wanted to bring by the flowers that my parents got for you. The balloons are from me and Stormy."

Not a hint of emotion from me. So he continued.

"I Came to check you out, you know?" He appeared a little uncomfortable. Probably because I was literally staring straight ahead as if I was a zombie, unable to comprehend the words that were coming out of his mouth.

"So anyway. When I first got the call about you being here… your sister told me you tried to hurt yourself in your mom's room and started buggin'. Yeah. Kyra said some shit like you found some old pictures of yourself and old police reports?"

Again he paused to study my face but he got nothing.

"I didn't know you was still trippin off that attack Shugar. But you gotta let it go. I got past it and I'm good. It's fucked up what happened to us but it's been ten years. Ain't no point in hashing up that old shit and making yourself end up here… you know?"

I was beginning to laugh and his discomfort in the inside. Regardless, I kept starting straight ahead until he sat on the edge of my bed. That's when I shot him a very evil look. You know that saying that if looks could kill…. Yeah that one. Rick would be dead twice over. It got his attention and he stood back up again and kept on talking.

"Well anyway Shugar. Umm. I told your sister-law that I would take Stormy to my parents until you was well enough to care of her." Rick moved closer to my bed and couldn't decide if I was paying him any attention at all.

"Alright then Shugar. I'ma bout to leave okay? I have some errands to run before I take our daughter out for dinner. You know... some Daddy-Daughter time." He chuckled nervously and finally backed out my room with a nervous shuffle.

19 JOURNAL ENTRY
July 7, 2000

Kyra was careful not to say to much as she drove me to my new condo in Montclair. I had only lived there a few weeks before I was hospitalized but I was extremely anxious to be in the luxury of my own bedroom and private space again.

Decorating Stormy's room to be every bit of pink, yellow, fluffy and soft as she had requested was on my list of a million things I wanted to do once I was settled in and comfortable.

My little sister was kind enough to stop at the beauty supply store and Target to pick up all the things I had explained to her that I required to go back home and not have to step back out to face the world again for a few more days. She had agreed of course with the notion that she'd be back the next morning to take me to my first doctor's follow-up visit in Livingston.

The first thing I did after Kyra had finally left me to the sanctity of my personal galaxy was cut all my hair. I cut my long beautiful silkened hair to within one inch of its life. Then I washed it with vinegar, conditioned it with mayonnaise and died it honey blonde.

Next, I emptied the closet of all my Jimmy Choo shoes and Louis Vuitton handbags and dumped them in three large thirteen gallon heavy duty trash bags and left them by my front door.

After I stacked all of the picture albums I had saved over the years, I neatly placed them in a large wood keep sake box that I purchased when Stormy was first born and kept all the best mementos of her I had collected.

When I had finally finished six of the seven things-to-do on my list, I took a long hot shower and poured myself into the royal blue and black bustier corset and matching panties I had purchased months ago for Nasir but never had an opportunity to wear. I painted my face with the new MAC palette I had never used before tonight and stared at myself in the mirror. Perfection! He is going to love this.

I carefully cut the hospital bandages and band from my wrists and camouflaged the scabs forming where I had cut myself, with liquid Band-Aid. I then placed two diamond tennis bracelets on each arm.

The silk Dolce and Gabana trench coat felt like the right amount of concealment on top to my almost naked brown skin as I drove to with the top down along the high way. I was enjoying how the wind felt on my scalp, rushing through my short natural curls. All eyes were on me in my brand new 740i royal blue convertible with a butter soft cream leather interior and wood paneling. Ha! I could give a fuck about any of these material things anymore. None of it mattered in this transformation I coined the 'authentic me'.

Pulling into this driveway, I noticed there were no other cars except his own. Good. He looked to be alone. Perfect.

Straightening my jacket so as not to reveal too much too fast I struck a pose and rang the bell. But for some reason, I became nervous. Maybe I shouldn't do this, I contemplated. However, that thought passed almost as fast as I thought it and I patiently waited for him to answer the door. I felt his presence on the other side of the door just as he turned the knob.

"DAMN! Shugar? What the... Damn!"

I grinned the bad girl's grin with my head tilted down but eyes glaring up; nibbling on my freshly manicured nails.

"Are you going to let me in?" I asked coyly.

"Hell yeah!" he stepped to the side.

I sashayed my very trim hips seductively by him and made trails with my eyes. I wanted him to shut the door and follow me into his living room.

When I heard the door shut behind us, I asked, "are you here alone?"

He was stuck looking me up and down in pure astonishment. I knew I had him and it didn't feel as good as I had hoped. Not yet anyway. Regardless, I was going to follow through with my plan to the letter because I had decided, tonight is the night; I've waited for this for far too long.

"Hello?" I waved my hand in front of his face to get his attention. "I asked if you were here alone." I repeated myself.

"Ummm.. yeah. I'm alone." He moved in close to my body and I felt his heat. Looking down at the growing bulge in his pants, I saw he was becoming aroused.

"Good." I said. I did my 'wonder-woman' stance and undid the belt to my jacket allowing the full allure of my toned body to be revealed.

"I was hoping we can talk. Is there somewhere we can sit and chit chat?"

I can see by the expression in his face the blood was beginning to travel to his brain again because the quizzical look was making its way down past his eyebrows and forming on his lips.

"Shugar. What are you doing here? When did you come home from the hospital? Are you even supposed to be out of the house? What do you want to talk about?" He was spitting out questions in rapid fire at me. But I knew how to shut him up and stop the interrogation. Besides, tonight was a long time coming.

"Do you still love me?" I was looking him straight in his eyes when I asked as I ignored his questions purposely.

Again, the puzzled look. "Yeah. Of course I do. I told you, I'ma always love you Shugar."

I leaned in and offered a quick kiss on his lips then I began to tug on his belt and zipper to his jeans. With a glimmer of hope in his eyes, his questionable thoughts were drowned out by the stiffness in his boxers while I began to massage his penis in my hands and he stood leaning against his foyer wall for support.

"Say please." My voice was low and guttural. I wanted him to want me bad.

"Please, Shugar."

Glaring in his eyes, breath hot against his cheek, I whispered, "I want to hear you say my entire name."

"Please.... aaaah... Cherise....Shugar....Brown."

"Where's your bedroom?"

"Upstairs to the right Cherise." Eyes glazed over, he

followed me to his bed. He wanted to jump right in but not yet, I thought.

"Stay standing." I commanded in my sex kitten voice. Slowly, I parted my legs and kneeled slowly, being sure to stop just as my face aligned with his crotch. I blew the head. He shivered with excitement.

"What would you have me do?

"Lick it!" he groaned.

"Ok. But not just yet."

I pulled his jeans all the way down, exposing his erection at full attention. He kicked them off and I stood back up, surprising him as I pushed him on the bed and joined him by climbing over his lap. I could literally see him pulsating. The veins in his length were tight against the skin. It looked like it hurt.

He arched his back and I wrapped my long legs around his waist. Then I leaned up on my knees while he aimed the mushroomed-capped appendage at my opening. But I pushed my breasts forwards towards his lips so distract him.

Greedily, he released my breasts from their lace jail and licked my nipples. I reached behind my back and pulled the small box cutter from the small of my back where it was quietly awaiting its assignment. I allowed a few more licks and groans to be exchanged between us before I slowly lifted his chin towards the ceiling and began a slow wet trail with my tongue from his navel. When the sharp blade of the box cutter reached his throat, I pushed the corner of it in, just before breaking the skin.

His eyes popped open but he couldn't form words to explain what he was feeling right then.

"Finally. This has been a long time coming and I was

wondering, how does it feel? Do you like this Rick?" I held the blade tight and whispered in his ear.

"How does it feel to be a victim? Feeling like you are at the mercy of somebody else's hands? My hands?" I teethed his earlobe with my front teeth.

I twisted around, maneuvering downward, positioning myself to witness the full view of his blossoming panic. I was feeling empowered and aroused myself in this moment. Feeling nothing but rage and excitement, I was looking forward to what is getting ready to happen.

Running my fingernails lightly across his scrotum, I stopped short and squeezed until my fingertips touched with his balls between them.

"You drove me to this Rick. Because of what you did to me, I wear scars like panty hose every day of my life. You set me up to be raped. And you deserve to feel violated and tormented like I did, don't you think?"

My demeanor was calm, steady and deliberate. I was asking questions callously while making small slices in the shaft of his penis. Seven slices; one for each rapist. He writhed in agony.

"Now you get to wear scars." I was remembering that girl Cherise as she awakened inside of me. Rick was releasing tears of fear and turmoil but I wasn't moved.

"Tell me why you did it Rick? Why was I gang raped? Hunh? Did you owe somebody money and you offered them me in exchange for payment?"

Exhaustedly, Rick moved his head from side to side to say no.

"That's not it? So then, you fucked up somebody's money and you set me up to get robbed to pay off your debt?"

"Let....let me..Shugar..let me explain what happened. They wasn't supposed to hurt you." He whined. "They was only supposed to take the money I told them you had. Shugar! I didn't mean for ..."

"Shut Up!?" I dragged the box cutter across Rick's forearm. He peed himself. Putting my face inches from his, I allowed Cherise to speak her mind.

"Don't try to explain shit to me motherfucker. You set me up and you knew it but decided to treat me like shit all these years. For what Rick? What did you get out of watching me cling to you like a lost puppy knowing you didn't love me back? And I was in love with you. I was stupid for you Rick. Nope. You can't explain yourself out of this."

Tears began to flood my eyes but it was Cherise crying, not me.

"For years, you knew what you did and you never said a damn thing about it. Instead you took pride in watching me unravel. Shrink into nothing. I tried to keep it together but when I found out that you, of all people, were the reason for my death.... All you can do for me now is die slow you bastard." I stabbed him in his thigh and dragged the blade down about seven inches.

"Shugar! Puh..please...don't!" Rick screamed out and begged for his life.

"Fuck you!"

I was growing tired of the game Cherise was playing with him. It's time to end this all right now. I pulled the cutter over my head and placed one hand around the other, fully hoping to plunge the entire thing deep into his chest.

"SHUGAR!" Ibin screamed from the bedroom door entrance.

I stopped the blade mid-air and turned in surprise. Ibin rushed towards me and tackled me as hard as he could off Rick's chest and onto the floor. Then he straddled me on the floor and wrestled the cutter out of my hands.

"What the fuck is wrong with you? You crazy? You about to kill this motherfucker!" Ibin was yelling at me with such force in his voice. He was angry and scared for me. I can tell. I said nothing. Just laid on the floor looking up at Ibin whom I hadn't seen in months.

Rick was standing on his feet again. Panting and backing himself into the farthest corner of the room. "Man! That bitch is crazy! Look what she did to me!"

POW! Ibin broke Rick's jaw with one punch.

"Get the fuck up and put your clothes on. We getting the fuck out of here!" He grabbed me by my arm and wrangled me to my feet. Ibin looked around the floor, fully expecting to find more female garments strewn about.

"That's all you wore over here? Girl.... Stand right here. Don't fucking move! You hear me?"

I shook my head slowly, yes.

Ibin turned towards Rick and noticed him still on the floor holding his jaw and trying to shake himself out of a daze.

"Yo punk ass better not NEVER tell another motherfucker what the fuck happened here tonight. If I ever hear about this shit from anybody on the fucking street, I swear on my father, I'ma cut your dick off myself and feed it to you!"

It wasn't until I felt Kyra awkwardly take my hand in

hers and guided me out of bedroom and out the door did I realize she was even there. She seemed afraid of me. Like she didn't recognize me or something.

My sister placed me in Ibin's truck and strapped me in before putting the child-safety lock on and shutting the passenger side door. She then walked around to the driver's side where Ibin was climbing in behind the wheel.

"I'ma take her car back to my house and park it there until you tell me what to do with it." She pauses before she finishes her thought.

"I just want to thank you Ibin for helping my sister. When I went back to her house and read her to do list and saw what she was planning to do to Rick, I didn't know who else to call. Shugar would have killed me if I had called Ethan to help. I. I'm just glad we got here in time and he didn't lock his front door. Anyway. I just wanted to say thank you."

Ibin shut his car door and left Kyra on the other side of it. "Look. I love Shugar and I would do anything for her…. Even save her crazy ass from herself. But I'ma need you to keep this between me and you only. Don't tell your brothers or your girlfriends cause shit about to get real out here. Okay? And you can trust I'ma take care of Shugar and make sure she alright. You can bank on that."

He put his hand on top of her hers that was resting in the window frame to reassure my sister that I was going to be okay. My sister walked back to my car and drove off in the opposite direction.

Ibin fidgeted in his seat, fastened his own seatbelt and put the truck in gear. As we began to leave Rick's street, he reached his right hand across the seat into my lap and took my hand.

The truck was quiet. The tinted windows made the cabin dark except for dim lighting coming from the dashboard. Ibin smoothed my hair and lovingly leaned over to kiss my cheek when we stopped at a light.

"You gonna be alright Shugar and everything I wrote in that note back in the day is gonna be true one day. But for now, I'm gonna get you some help."

20 JOURNAL ENTRY
July 10, 2000

When NPD arrived at Ibin's home, they hit with what felt like a million questions.

"When was the last time you spoke to Cherise Brown?"

He answered, "I haven't seen or spoken to Shugar since the day of her mother's funeral. I sat with her at the cemetery for a lil' while after everybody left then I took her home."

The officers studied his face as they spoke and tried to look around Ibin into his apartment but he had the door barely opened and he was smart enough to use his frame to block their view. I hate these bastards!

"Did you know she was in the hospital a couple of weeks ago?"

"Yeah. Everybody knew that. And?"

"And! Everybody also knows you have a major love for this woman… you didn't go visit her in the hospital?"

"No."

"Why not?

He became hesitant to answer at first. Not wanting to speak to loudly for hustling ears, he nervously lit a cigarette and talked a bit lower.

"Well, because…. I don't do hospitals and because I didn't want to run into her husband. Plus. I just didn't want to see her like that."

"And you haven't spoken to..uh….Shugar since the hospital visit right?"

"No Officer. I said I haven't seen or spoken to Shugar since her mother's funeral".

"Are you sure Ibin? Are you sure you haven't heard or seen Ms. Brown in the last past couple of days?"

"What do mean, am I sure? Hell yeah, I'm sure. If you got something to say about Shugar then say it but don't play with my intelligence with all these bullshit-ass questions."

The cop didn't want to come out and state anything that would tip him off to why there were really at his house or what they were investigating. There were six cops standing outside his apartment; five too many to not be making any arrests.

A second officer decided it was his turn to interrogate but he had a different inquisitive tone to his voice than the first.

"Mr. James, do you happen to be related to or know a Matthew James?"

"Hunh?" Ibin stalled. I can tell he wasn't expecting that question at all.

"He went by the name Bull?.... did you know him?"

"What does that have to do with anything Officer? I thought you were asking me questions about seeing or hearing from Shugar. What does Matthew James have to do with those questions?"

"Ironically Mr. James, a lot." He paused as he began to ponder the connections he thinks he just made.

"You see, Matthew James was, at one point, considered to have been involved with the rape of a one Cherise Shugar Brown a couple of years ago but he was never brought up on charges. I remember that case and the victim especially because at the time, I had a daughter the same age as she. So, you can imagine my eagerness to drive to this very apartment those many years ago to talk to that Mr. James about his involvement. I was always so sure that purp had a lot to do with that brutal attack on her but no one ever turned over on him."

"Okay." was Ibin's only reply. He began shifting his weight from one foot to the other. Even I can tell that statement makes him uncomfortable.

"Well, I ask if you knew that Mr. James because this happens to be the same apartment he lived in and it's where a different Mr. James lives now. Because your last name is James; his last was James. We are talking about the same Cherise Brown who was the victim then and who we want to talk too now and finally because at the time I questioned that Mr. James, he had a son that was around 13, 14, 15 years old. And you look a lot like that Mr. James would look like if he was still alive. A lot of coincidences don't you think Ibin James?"

"Look! I haven't seen or heard from Shugar and if you have any more questions pertaining to her, you might want to talk to her family. Otherwise, I'm done with all these questions."

When Ibin finally closed the door and turned to face me, I was sitting on the floor of his living room area. He wasn't sure what to say to me. He stood staring for a least a minute formulating a thought that would ease whatever pain he thought I was feeling.

I stood up slowly from the floor as he walked towards the window, ensuring the police had left. It didn't matter to me just yet that the police were looking for me or that Rick might have pressed charges for what I did to him.

"Ibin?"

"Yeah?"

"Do you know Matthew James? Bull?"

"Shugar don't worry about all that right now. We need to be figuring out how we gon' keep your ass from getting' locked up."

"Ibin….. do you know who Bull is?"

"I swear to God, I'ma end up killing your boy Rick for doing just what I told him not to do. Rat ass nigah!"

"Ibin? Please do not ignore me or my questions. Do you know who Matthew Bull James is?"

He flops down on his couch and lets out a deep sigh as if he is defeated.

"Shugar. I do know who Matthew James is."

"Okay."

"Matthew James is my father."

Now I'm on the couch releasing deep sighs of astonishment. I turned in my corner of the couch to face Ibin straight on. I needed to see his face as he explained all this too me.

"You knew who Matthew James was all this time and you never told me? You knew all about his involvement in the attack on me Ibin and you were smiling in my face? In my brother's face, like it's all good?"

"I didn't know he had anything to do with that shit that

happened to you until just after I met you and started talking to you. When my mother started to see how I was feeling towards you, she sat me down one day and tried to explain to me what she thought his involvement was. But what she told me and what different people who use to run with him told me don't exactly add up so I decided to not say anything about it."

There was a look of terror in his eyes and in the sound of his words. He couldn't trust that what he was telling me wouldn't turn me against him forever.

"See. This is the kind of shit that makes me start to hate all the men in my life. The fact that you knew all along that your own father was entangled, and I don't care how much or how little, and you didn't tell me from the beginning of you calling yourself my friend… makes me not trust you anymore."

He didn't know what to say or do in this moment and neither did I. But I knew how I felt and it was a crushing feeling. Just as I began to trust this man, like him even, I find out that he can't be trusted by me at all.

"Ibin, I appreciate you helping me with the Rick problem I have on my hands right now and for keeping me safe these past couple of days but I think it's time for me to go and deal with the mess I've created."

'Where you goin' Shugar?"

"I don't know yet but I have to find a place that I can be by myself for a while and figure out the rest of my life. Need to put all this in perspective for once; who is for me or against me and to do that I need to create peace. Peace within and peace with all the wrongs that have been done with me. You understand?"

"Do you need anything? Money?"

"No. I don't want anything from you right now Ibin. I think you have done enough."

"I'ma be here when you need me Shugar. Always."

AUGUST 13, 2000
5:36 pm

RING! RING!

"You have reached the voicemail system for Doctor Regina Allen of the Mental Health and Wellness Center. No one is available to take your call right now but please leave a detailed message at the sound of the beep and someone will contact you at the earliest convenience...... BEEP."

"Oh. Hello. My name is Cherise Shugar Brown and I was hoping to make an appointment to talk to Doctor Allen..... Rising Phoenix Rape Clinic referred me to you. (pause) I was raped. Well, that's not all... I was ganged raped a while ago and I always thought I was okay. That I had rose above my circumstance and moved along in my life. Except I haven't. After almost ten years of holding all the hurt and pain inside so that my family and friends would be okay with what happened to me, I've begun to unravel. My entire family has been affected by this except we all pretended we weren't.

Dr. Allen, I need to tell it. I need to tell it all to someone. My story, my life, in its entirety has been exhausting, draining and completely fulfilling.

Finally, I need someone to just listen to me intently and allow me moments to grieve myself. My past self; Cherise. Even my current self...Shugar.... My mother's brown sugar cube. Ha! More like a melted sugary mess.

Anyway, I have journals Doctor Allen! I kept most of my life hidden behind bound books and notes to myself. I did that to release. To be able to mind-dump... From the day I was attacked until now... it's in all writing. And I'm finally ready to share it.. to talk about it.

RPR insisted that you are the best psychotherapist in the area and if I'm going to ever get custody of my daughter back, you are the person to make that happen.

So. Can you help me?"

AUGUST 8, 2002
(RICK)

Before leaving her mother's house, I was making a second attempt at begging Cherise to please let me take her first payroll check and 'invest' it so that I can make us some money. It was all I could do to secretly talk her into helping me out of the mess I had gotten myself into without telling her the truth.

Instead I told her the money the she let me use to 'invest' in a short time ROTH IRA would be money that we'd use as seed money to start our lives together when we were both done with college.

But it was her first check as a full-time employee with the insurance company she had been working at as a high school intern. She was so proud that they thought so much of her to keep her on after graduating high school and enrolling in a local college that she made her own plans for her first paycheck.

Cherise was going to take that cashed check, turn it into a money order and make her first payment towards the interest on a student loan. A loan she had just received and where interest payments or otherwise wouldn't need to paid until she finished school or dropped out. -- Her classes hadn't even started yet!

With her mind made up, she said no to my idea. Shugar tried to convince me that paying back loans and keeping interests rates down now would benefit our impending nuptials later in life.

I decided to let it go because I had a second plan in place; one I was trying to avoid. Yet, Shugar is leaving me no choice. Besides, it has gotten too late to call it off.

It's about 8:30 at night and Cherise and I are strolling from her mother's house to my house. My parents were still living on Priceland Avenue at the time.

Whenever Cherise and I were anywhere in public together, she always got a lot of attention from men and women. Standing at five feet eleven inches, slender but shapely frame, beautiful large almond shaped eyes; skin the color of oatmeal cookies and the prettiest smile you'd ever want to see… Everyone always told her she should be a model but it wasn't in her nature to garner that kind of attention for herself. Instead, she was laid back and quaint.

Her mother didn't allow her to do much outside the house so she was very naïve to the streets. Besides leaving with one of her brothers or me, she never hung out in the neighborhood much or made many friends. That's why I felt a little bad for what was to happen.

When I saw them approaching, I was kind of wishing I can make it stop before it got started. I had a gut feeling that somehow, this was going to turn out the way it was strategized. Something about how Smalls was leading his pack and staring directly in my eyes as he was walking towards Cherise and I made me grab her hand and pull her in the street away from what I now knew was going to be danger.

As the last of Bull's team of thugs were passing by Cherise, I thought for sure they decided to not go through with the scheme and I was relieved.

But then I feel my girlfriend being pulled away from me and I knew it was going down for sure.

With the force of her pocketbook being snatched off her I'm immediately turned around. So I grab her hand tighter and pull her closer into me so she doesn't get away.

The idea was for them to snatch the purse, take the cash out and run with it. All I had to do was pretend to be just as surprised as she was, throw a few air punches like I'm defending her but allow them to get away with the money. Except it didn't happen that way.

Instead, Smalls pulls her arm and hand out of my grip and slams her to the ground. And when I go to talk to ask one of the guys what was going on and explain this wasn't part of what was plotted, I was hit in the face with a pole.

I'm being punched in the head and kicked in the stomach while someone else is literally ripping the pockets off my pants, exposing my legs. Every time I try to speak, I'm hit a again and again.

Lying about five feet from Cherise, she and I are both on the ground but I realize they are tearing off her clothes piece by piece. All the while I'm being spit on and robbed of the thirty-five hundred cash I had took from my father's stash. That money was going to be added to the fifteen hundred they were supposed to take from her. Then, I was going to give the entire five-thousand to Bull to give to Pac Man as a payoff of my debt. At that point I would be out of the game. Forever.

That's when I realized that Bull wasn't even among the group of men whooping my ass.

"What the fuck is going on?" I managed to yell out in between hits to my ribs with a stick and punches to my eyes and jaw.

"Oh you wanna know what's going on lil' niggah?"

"What's going is we robbing yo punk ass and fucking your girl! That's what's going on." Smalls eyes were dark and criminal. If I didn't already know him, I'd swear he didn't have two different colored eyes.

"Since Bull decided he could scab us out to do the fucking job Pac Man paid him to do, we decided that bullshit money he offered us ain't half of what you got in your motherfuck'n pockets so we paying our self and letting that niggah figure out what to tell his boss!"

I was fucked and I knew it! I looked over at Cherise and I couldn't even tell if she was still breathing. Her eyes are opened and but she's staring up at the sky. Not moving, making no noise; not even whimpering anymore.

When I noticed two of the seven whip out his penis and start pissing her face and mouth, I tried hard to reach her. My instinct was to protect her from that kind of assault. It was my initial intention to try to fight these guys off of her. THIS is not what was supposed to happen. The most that was ensure upon her is that she would end up with a scrapped knee or something. Not this!

But I couldn't get to her at all. I was still being held down and forced to watch them punch, kick and bite her all over her body. They were enjoying watching her face swell and her eyes close from the beating she was getting. At one point, they almost came to blows over whose turn it was to rape her again.

I was sick to my stomach and began to throw-up on the two that held me down. I was released from their clutches as they joined the others.

With a broken leg, bruised ribs and a black eye, I stayed still on the ground long enough to watch as her legs were spread apart and a soda can was shoved inside her.

She screamed! Her voice returned as she began yelling, 'Fire, Fire, Fire....' At least she was still alive.

When I noticed that they had all began to run away, I climbed to my feet and limped and skipped as fast as I could in the opposite direction. Too afraid to approach her; to help her in fear they told her I was a part of this.

I had only made it about a block away when my senses came back to me and I decided to go back and bring her out of that field. I needed to get her to a hospital. And just as I was going to re-enter the lot where Cherise was still lying half-naked and crying, I noticed an old lady approach her with a blanket so I limped back behind the house as crowds of people began to gather.

It wasn't until I saw that her older brother Ethan had arrived did I decide to leave the scene altogether. He'd make sure she was okay. Besides, I felt every inch like the asshole I was for setting this whole thing up to begin with. How was I going to explain to Cherise that what happened to her wasn't supposed to happen?

While my parents were out for the night, I found my way home and cleaned myself up the best I could. Every time the room became still however, I would see Cherise being violated, over and over in my mind. I began to cry out loud and beat on myself for not being man enough to try to fight back for her. I could have taken one of them down!

But then I thought about it. -- I saw Smalls had a gun in his waist and if I had attempted to do anything but lay down like the coward I was and take the beating and robbery, he would have shot both of us.

After two fat blunts and a fifth of Hennessy, the nightmare in my head wouldn't stop playing. So I decided to take a trip to the 'spot' and approach Pac Man about what went down. The worst that could happen is that he kills me on the spot and that did not matter right now; I deserved it.

My drunken mouth spoke a sober truth when I told the biggest dope dealer in a forty block radius that his goons were foul and deserved every unsavory thing that was sure to come their way for what they did to Cherise Brown.

I was surprised at the outrage Pac Man displayed when he heard the news. He was aware of the robbery that was supposed to happen and the total sum of five-thousand dollars he was to receive that night to pay off my own debt. But apparently, Bull never communicated to him to say he wouldn't be there to keep his soldiers on their leashes. Not to mention, that no one told him that the Cherise that was going to be robbed was Cherise Shugar Brown; Sheila Robert's child. His daughter!

I left Pac Man's stash house with almost ten-thousand dollars in cash and a verbal contract with this imp to never tell a soul what I had just learned. The new deal on the table was to have the seven men who raped Cherise arrested and I would help to testify against them. In exchange, I would receive another ten-thousand dollars and each defendant would receive a death sentence upon release from prison as an added sentence on top of whatever the courts bestowed.

But when Cherise ended up pregnant with Stormy, I got a 'kite' from Pac Man warning me take care of his grandchild and claim her as my own; even if I had doubts. Of course I was reminded to not repeat what I knew about him and Cherise's mother. I complied.

Fast forward almost ten years and I'm feeling like revenge, as far as I'm concerned, is best served cold. And that's exactly what Miss Brown has been receiving for the past two years. An ice cold serving of retribution for what she did to me.

Having the courts grant my parents full custody of Stormy because her crazy ass fell off her damn rocker was the best thing that could have happened! It's unfortunate that they wouldn't give me custody because they wanted to investigate her claim of my little part in the attack on her.

Really, I don't care. Well, I do because that bitch has my parents looking at me sideways ever since because of the lies Shugar has been spewing out about me. My parents never needed to know that I was even questioned in regards to that attack on BOTH OF US.

As far as they knew, I was a victim just like she was and the only reason I had talked to the police or made those few court appearances was to assist in putting those criminals behind bars. For my part, one jacked-up plan to get money does a criminal make!

They never knew about my failed attempts to be a street pharmacist or that I was concerned about them being able to afford to send me college at all. And at the time of all of this happening, they felt sorry enough for both Shugar and I to take out a second mortgage on their home just to ensure that I could finish all four years of college and stay away from the 'riff-raff' that had attacked Shugar and me.

When Stormy was born, they took it upon themselves to step up as co-parents on my behalf. They wanted to make sure that if they put the time and effort into Stormy while I was away at school, I'd have no need to drop out and possibly get caught up in the streets. They lost one son that way, and didn't want to take chances with only remaining son.

My mother was a high school principal before she retired and she had come across many of her students who were brilliant thinkers; one's she thought would make great college students. The issue, however, always came down to them falling victim to their surroundings, parents who worked too much and didn't put interest in their children's future or merely that they had no hopes of aspirations to reach beyond their circumstance. She saw her own mistakes as a parent in them.

Regardless, I turned out fine. Entering my second year of college was tough financially on my parents so I thought hustling would relieve some of their stress. Luckily, Shugar became pregnant and they never knew about this part of my life... until now.

But I have many more exact ways to get back at her for all the mess she brought to the forefront. The next thing I plan to do is ensure that Miss Brown receives an invitation to my impending wedding to Trina. I know she won't be in attendance, but at the very least, it should make her very jealous and envious.

Shugar still wants me. She always will. And knowing that she can never have me back will crush her ratchet ass! It will fuck with what's left of her mind even though she'll run around pretending that fact isn't bothering her.

After all, she tried to be married and look what happened to that union. FAILED. Every relationship she has been in has been a failure and she would blame all that on me of course.

I don't care how much therapy she seeks or how many 'survivor' meetings she attends. She will never be considered well enough to be a fit parent if I have anything to do with it. I will stop her at every turn.

That bitch carved me up like a grilled steak and I'm supposed to forgive her just because she some kind of victim of rape? Fuck that! No!

And when she starts begging me to not marry Trina and get back with her, you know what I'ma do? I'ma have an affair with that whore and fuck her brains out! I'ma have her simple behind dick-whipped just like I know she had that young dude Ibin pussy-whipped. I plan to do to her what she did to him and have her licking my Adidas like the dog she is.

I will bone her every day if I have to and make sure she end up pregnant again. Except this time, it won't be any doubt in anybody's mind that this baby will be by me.

I hate looking into Stormy's face all the time and not seeing any kind of reflection of me or my family. Its gut-wrenching hearing her call me Daddy and half the damn time I'm unsure if that title is correct.

It's a real fucked up thing that happened to Shugar and it was poor timing that Stormy was conceived in the middle of that craziness. And I know it's not anyone's fault that the question of who is Stormy's father has plagued us for the past nine years.

Now that she is coming of age, my little princess is starting to ask a lot of questions and it hasn't always been easy trying to make sense of everything she has witnessed in her young life. Yet, it's another opportunity to start spoon feeding her the real truth about her mother.

Oh, I'll do it little doses here and there, but the sooner I get her to see her to see her tramp mother for who she is, the more I'll feel like I got my just do.

In the meantime, knowing that her daughter will eventually be raised in my house with my new wife should finally should fuck her head a little more. And to add insult to injury I might just hint at telling her who her real father is; that should send her over the edge. The rest, she'll do on her own.

AUGUST 8, 2002
(IBIN)

We stood in sinking mud while it poured heavy raindrops upon our heads. I held my mother's hand very tight when I noticed the black Hurst Cadillac enter the cemetery where the large crowd of people had gathered. Everyone who was there was dressed in black; they created a direct path to the large opening in the ground where he would rest in peace for eternity.

As they removed my father's coffin, my mother buckled to her knees. The pain that filled her heart when it became apparent she had lost forever, the only one she had ever loved.

Just the Tuesday before, I heard my parents argue about all the crimes that were being whispered about in the neighborhood. Particularly, they were discussing the gang of my father's 'associates' who jumped on some girl and raped her. My mother was complaining loudly that my father's involvement was making her very uncomfortable and that she didn't want him to work for or being around those kinds of people anymore.

She was making it a point to tell him that they had

always made a way after he was laid off from his construction job. That being the 'strong-arm' for drug dealers, carrying guns and acting as security for these types of characters to keep his family fed was not something she could accept. She wanted him to stop.

My father wasn't the kind of man who yelled or cursed at his woman. He never raised his voice or his hands to her no matter how upset he was or what she had done to provoke him. In fact, he despised any male who would disrespect any woman in any way. And if they didn't hold all women in general in high regard, they deserved no good fortune.

But this specific argument with my mother, he was passionate about. He pleaded with her to understand that he didn't have anything to do with what happened to that girl and that he was home with us because I was sick and she had to work. He tried to help her understand that although he had heard about and was part of the initial plan, he knew some things about that incident that he just couldn't talk to her about. She just had to trust him.

He wanted her to know where he was coming from and to get onboard with his hustling strategies. My father wanted badly for her to understand that he needed to be the man who took care of his family.... even if it meant he had to do some down-low and dirty things. If it meant he had to be involved with drug dealers and protect them from the always impending street wars to feed his family and pay the bills then he was insistent that is what he would continue to do.

My father needed my mother to get onboard, otherwise he wouldn't be able to hustle and bring home money knowing it was making her upset and she'd reject it and him.

My mother, Mona, wasn't hearing any of it and she

called him a coward. That's when he punched a hole in the wall as large as his ape sized fist.

My father, Bull, had turned into his namesake in that instant and angrily drove away from the house; neither of them knowing that he would never live to see another day.

A few hours later, I sat watching wrestling when the noise of someone banging on our door startled me and my mother. At first, I wasn't so sure what my father's best friend was yelling when he said, there had been a shooting and Bull had been shot.

"Why?! Why?!" I heard my mother cry out as I ran to the door with tears in my own eyes; unsure of what was actually going on. Yet, somehow I knew my father wasn't coming back. Ever.

I ear hustled the conversation between my mother and Ray as he explained that Bull was shot twice in the face and stomach and that he she needed to come down to the corner to see for herself.

My mother and I rushed to the corner and pushed through the crowd and there; I saw my father lying on the ground, eyes still open, staring into the sky. Blood had puddled around his body.

In his hands he was clutching a Universal Sneaker store bag that held a brand new pair of Air Jordan V's in my size, a can of my mother's favorite chocolate candy, Katy Dids and six of her favorite flower; the crab-apple rose.

At that moment, all innocence escaped me and my life as a child ended. I had to be the man of the house now and take care of my mother. It was me, now, who is charged with doing-what-I-have-to-do to make sure she and I were okay.

That's what Bull taught me; to be a man first and take care of your family above all else. 'By any means necessary' is what he always preached.

"There is always calm after the storm and that's when you make time for yourself." he'd say. "To re-organize, plan and plot to find your way out of the next storm that was always sure to come."

I remembered that he had always made it plain to me that if anything ever happened to him, then I was to step into the role of bull-of-the-den the very second he shut his eyes for good.

Kneeling on the ground next to my dad, I kissed him on the cheek and ran my palm down his face, closing his eyes forever. Then I stood up and took my mother by her hand and lead her back to the house. As we walked away, the ambulance had arrived and quickly determined he was going to be DOA. It was when they draped the white sheet over his body that I became a man.

When Kyra called me to tell me that she thought for sure Shugar had gone to Rick's house after leaving the hospital, it was all I could do to get to her before someone got hurt.

And when I walked in on her, blade in hand and ready to plunge it into his chest.... My gut reaction was to tackle her crazy ass to the floor.

I thought about Stormy in those first moments and what it would mean for her to lose her dad in an act of violence. The way I had lost my own. I knew the pain she would suffer for the rest of her life would be hard on her and I couldn't let that happen.

Don't get me wrong; I love Shugar. I've always loved Shugar and probably will always love her but it's no way I could let her take that man's life even if he did deserve it.

I should explain. I couldn't let her do it for a few reasons. First, she is a female and she has been hurt. Hurt badly. A woman scorned ain't nothing to be fucked with. But I have some things I need to talk to Rick about myself before anybody puts him out for the count. Namely, about my father and what he knows about Bull.

As of right now, Shugar needs Rick to get custody of her daughter back and that's gonna be an uphill battle considering she is in therapy for a mental breakdown.

At the same time, I need to put more focus into my own seed right now. And I'm reminded again of that fact, when I found a picture of the two of us in the kitchen drawer.

I am holding her about five minutes after birth; she fit neatly in my two hands. Wow! She was so damned little.

I remember how my heart fit so perfectly around her little finger – small as it was. It is a long time ago but she still has me wrapped around her now two year old fingers! I've always been.

On the day my heart was born, I remember I took her from her mother's arms while she cried tears of pain and joy. She was so upset still with me but at the same time we were being bonded together for life… she wasn't sure she wanted that. And in her mumbled prayers she was asking God to create for our daughter, a father that would be everything she wished she had.

To ease the pain of my daughter's mother, I spoke softly into my baby girl's ear, "You will always be this child here in my hands. I will never leave you nor forsake you. I love you Isis. One day, if it's God will, you will know how deeply my love for you goes. It's already a bottomless vein in my heart. And I will tell to you as my father has told it to me: as you grow up, you will find yourself in the darkness of your own pains. At first you'll feel all alone but then you'll reach down inside yourself and suddenly feel a foundation beneath you...it will be me!"

I vowed from that day that I became a father to be everything to mine what my father was to me but so much better. This is why I'm on this journey to learn the truths about who my father was and why he died; so I'm never prone to repeat his past.

AUGUST 8, 2002
(CHERISE SHUGAR BROWN)

Dear Mother,

When I was a child I looked up to you and sought out your
approval and acceptance. I wanted nothing more than to love
you; and to be loved by you. I wanted to be held in your arms and
feel the comfort of your protectiveness. For the first twelve years
I felt you were always doing your best with me and because I had
nothing else to compare it too, I determined for myself that I felt
loved from you.

Ethan, Jamil and Jamal were your 'kings' and you treated
them as such. They wanted for nothing and at first I was your
little princess. Always in the finest clothes, beautiful Sunday
dresses and shoes; dance classes and recitals; gymnastics and
tumbling. You were building well-rounded children and that was
commendable considering the city we grew up in.

In return for feeling loved, I gave you all the unconditional
adoration I could muster to show you I was worthy of all you
were providing me; us.

However, your disdain for me was progressive as I developed
into womanhood. Everyone saw it but no one spoke on it. And

by the time I was sixteen, it became painfully apparent that for all of my absolute devotion to you, it wasn't enough.

When Kyra was born, it was painfully clear that you had certain contempt for me particularly. Now that there was another female born to the 'throne' of Sheila Roberts, there was now something to equate your love too. You grew to hate me.

You began to want more from me than a child was expected to give. I needed to be perfect at everything and invisible at the same time. You barely let me outside after a certain age and claimed it was because 'all the kids in the neighborhood were bad' and you didn't want me to be so-called influenced by them. I couldn't have friends over from school and I certainly would never ask if I could go to their homes.

In fact, you discouraged me from even making friends at all. No sleepovers, no parties, no play dates. No mates at all. I often wondered if your heart enjoyed what your mind did to my psyche before that brutal attack ever happened because you tapped into that part of my brain so many times.

By the time I met Rick, I was so naïve about men, people, and our life outside your house. I became Rick's prey so easily because I didn't know better. When he started showing me any kind of attention in high school, I was overjoyed that someone could see me. I wasn't invisible to him. I wasn't a figment of my own imagination.

Rick was the first person to touch my slender body and tell me I was attractive. At fifteen years old, he was the first to notice that my hips began to spread slightly and my breasts were developing. Once when I panicked about menstruating, he calmed my nerves and explained to me that it wasn't as 'bad' a thing like what you had drilled into my head. As long as I wasn't sexually active then I had no worries. Mom. I didn't lose my virginity to Rick until I was 18 years old!

As a teenager and an adult I become attracted to what I knew… mental abuse. So Rick was everything I thought I needed. Except he was everything I should have avoided.

I was so unaware of life outside of your house or school that unbeknownst to me Mother, you inadvertently taught me how to survive in spite of my circumstances. That was a blessing.

When you're made to feel like you are always scratching and scheming to stay on top of the food chain, you learn to make a way for yourself. To come home every day, as a young girl, to a mother who showed envy towards my innocence was unnerving.

I learned how to ignore your whispers whenever you were in one of your 'moods'; a state of trance, re-living your own hurts and pains. As soon as you were filled up with agony from your memories, you'd pour them on me. You tried to drown me in your own pitifulness and self-hatred. You cursed me and loathed my birthdate time and time again only to show me moments of regret for the way you KNEW you were behaving towards me.

When I entered your room that day after your death and I trashed it…. there were flashbacks: You barging into the bathroom, pushing me off the toilet, snatching the pregnancy test out of my hand, throwing it in my face and calling me a whore for being pregnant after the rape.

I swallowed my pain and the filthy ways you made me feel down to my core the entire time I was pregnant with Stormy. I was so furious with you. I wanted to scream, but you looked so sick in those kinds of moments. You were so pathetic. I always swallowed my hatred for you and practiced being unseen just so I could avoid those instances from happening again.

As a young child I thought I must have done something wrong, that it was my fault that you disliked me so much. And by the time I was a teenager I was used to it, and tried taking it with a grain of salt.

I've tried reasoning with myself over the years, that you had your own problems, and when I finally understood that you were a victim of rape as well, I knew you used the emotional abuse you bestowed upon me to mask your own tears.

I have to pause right here…. truthfully that's some bullshit and that excuse doesn't hold water. It doesn't change the fact that you did these things to your own child. You should have sought help for yourself so that you could help me. Even better, you should have allowed me to receive the help you didn't get so I wouldn't be like you!

Yet enough is enough and though I'll never forgive you for allowing my brother to beat my ass while you sat back and watched in glee, I can now take solace in knowing it wasn't my fault that you were the way you were. That even though you're my mother, that maybe it's okay to despise every wretched and vile part of you that didn't love me.

I have tried so hard to hate you, but I can't. I have tried so hard to convince myself that I no longer love you, but again I fail. I have tried so hard to have an unsure opinion of you. Yet on every level I still love you. Perhaps that's because I was never able to let go of the unconditional love I had for you.

It was always an issue of all the ruined relationships I've had. They all failed to understand that the emotional abuse I experienced with you coupled with the gang rape did this to me. It damaged me in ways you wouldn't understand unless you speak with another survivor.

For the first time in years I am finally feeling real love from a man and I'm learning how to receive it. It's taking me time to trust him and what his presence in my life means, but I'm trying.

My therapist, Dr. Allen, is a gift. He gave me back that last tatter of my former self, Cherise. She was still inside me, hiding in the dark, legs curled to her body, head down and door barricaded - protecting the last shred of her heart. He took her hand and led her to the tree house that the man she knew as her father, built for her in his own backyard, her most connected and safe place and brought light into her world.

Dr. Allen gave me permission to finally read the letter you wrote me a few days before you died.

You talked about how you were molested and raped as a child and adult. That you were that way with me to protect me from the kinds of torture you knew. You apologized. You stated you always loved me; differently. And you vowed the legacy of tortuous living ended with me - - and it has.

My children are my life and, God forbid, something like this happened to them, they will able talk to me about it until the day I die. Because I know – holding it in, forgetting about it, pretending it didn't happen, only makes them a victim over and over again. I won't ever allow that to happen. Not to either Stormy or Isis.

It is easy to love them unconditionally and it's always been easy to express. I know now that there has been no greater form of unconditional love then a parent toward their children.

Today Mommy, I'm getting the help I should have received many years ago. I'm learning that I can be better and I can be strong. I'm releasing the pain I felt from you. I'm forgiving you and I'm letting you go. I'm telling you that it wasn't your fault either. What happened to you made you the way you were and I wish someone had saved you from yourself.

If you were here now I'd recite to you what my survivor group starts every meeting with, "remember – you survived – you have strength – there are people who can help and I am one of them."

I love you Mommy! I burn this letter hoping the words turns to the ashes that reaches your soul in heaven.

xoxoxo ~ your BrownShugar

Next Book:

THE STORM AFTER THE CALM

BROWNSHUGAR II

YOLANDA HUGHES

THANK YOU 'FRIEND'

To my very special 'Friend'. Thank you will never be enough for being my friend for the past 19 years and counting. When all things changed around us and too us individually, you remained steadfast throughout. I can stand witness to the fact that men like you exist in this world. As far as I'm concerned, you are the personification of the word MAN and I blame your parents for having raised such a caring, protective and loving person. I have no idea what it feels like to not be loved by someone in this world because YOU always just loved me; for whoever I was in any given moment and I'm so very grateful for that. Your friendship has gotten me through my darkest hours and it's because of you, I am healed. I continue to pray that you remain constant in my life until we are both no more.

And to my Father art in Heaven... YOU are and therefore I am....BrownShugar!

Thank you!

NOTE FROM THE AUTHOR

Writing BrownShugar has been a life-long passion of mine that I've been working on accomplishing for many, many years. I've sought advice from friends and family on how to approach certain topics and reaction to particular things and everyone had been so humbling in their sharing.... They cheered me on encouraged me along the way. And so here she is in all her glory and spoken truths. BrownShugar.

Throughout the process, many have asked if Shugar is based on a real character and to that I say that Shugar is a character in this series. She does not live in the physical form however, there are so many Shugar's in the world that someone needed to tell her story. I was charged with that task.

Shugar, Rick and Ibin were not written to be heroes, idols or villains. However, they were all written to be real, relatable and honest in their emotions as well as their reactions. That is what I want every reader to walk away with.

As I work on the remaining books of this trilogy, I make a promise to stay true to each character as they develop, mature and grow throughout their life events. In the interim, I thank you for joining the ride and I look forward to your feedback. **I Am BrownShugar!**

Author,
Yolanda Hughes

xoxoxo
Yolanda

BrownShugar | **Enterprise**

Visit the author at

www.brownshugar.com

or contact her at

brownshugar713@gmail.com

Janet P. Suggs | *Book Manager for BrownShugar Enterprise* |
862.253.8015 or JSuggs@gmail.com

Yolanda Hughes
(973) 280-8262.
yhughes713@gmail.com

ABOUT RAPE

Rape can happen to anyone; children, students, wives, mothers, working women, grandmothers, the rich and poor, boys and men.

Myth: Rape is about sex and passion.
FACT: Rape is an act of violence. It is an attempt to control and degrade using sex as a weapon.

Myth: Most rapes are committed by strangers.
FACT: It is estimated that 80% of rapes are committed by someone the victim knows.

Myth: Rape is an impulsive, uncontrollable act of sexual gratification.
FACT: Most rapes are planned. Studies show that between 60 to 75 % of rapes are planned in advance of attacking victims.

Myth: Only young, beautiful women are raped.
FACT: Rapists of both sexes (male and female) attack women, children and men of all races, all ages and without regard to physical appearance.

If you or someone you know is a victim of rape, I encourage you to seek help immediately.

National Sexual Assault Hotline
1.800.656.HOPE(4673)
FREE. CONFIDENTIAL. 24/7.

Made in the USA
Charleston, SC
11 April 2014